Stop Reading, Start Studying:

Inductive Bible Study Method Explained

Vance,
Thanks for your
support!
Henry

Henry Jackson III

Ordering Information:

Quantity sales. Special discounts are available on quantity purchases by non-profits, ministries, churches, corporations, associations, and others. For details, contact the publisher via email at sales@inductivebiblestudyapp.com.

Printed in the United States of America

First Printing, 2015

ISBN
Paperback: 978-0-9970743-0-7
Kindle: 978-0-9970743-1-4
ePub: 978-0-9970743-2-1
Audiobook: 978-0-9970743-3-8

www.inductivebiblestudyapp.com

Because of the dynamic nature of the internet, any web addresses or links contained in this book may have changed since publication and may no longer be valid.

All Scripture quotations, unless otherwise noted, are taken from: **New** American Standard Bible®, Copyright © 1960, 1962, 1963, 1968, 1971, 1972, 1973, 1975, 1977, 1995 by The Lockman Foundation. Used by permission. (www.Lockman.org)

D o you love the Inductive Bible Study method and wish you could do it wherever you go? Introducing the Inductive Bible Study App (InductiveBibleStudyApp.com). This one-of-a-kind app empowers individuals to grow in their faith by enabling them to study the Bible inductively using their favorite mobile or tablet device. With this app, you can:

- *Mark Key Words* - Use images, and highlight, bold or italicize text (and more) for easy visual reference.

- *Take Notes* - Journal your personal study of the Scriptures and reflect on your growth.

- *Apply Themes* - Specify the theme of each chapter and even group verses together with division themes.

- *Perform Word Studies* - Understand the words of the Bible in their original language via the built-in Strong's concordance.

- *Research Cross References* - Discover every instance that a word is used in the Bible to gain a comprehensive understanding of it.

Download the #1 Free Inductive Bible Study App today!

DEDICATION

To my Lord and Savior Jesus Christ - this is yet another feeble attempt to make disciples of all nations...teaching them to observe all that You command.

To my queen, Vanessa. Thank you for your constant support and encouragement. God couldn't have blessed me with a better "help-meet" to share my life with. And to our prince Henry IV - although it may be years before you are able to read this book, each night as I listen to you pray by your bedside, I am filled with joy as you pray God's blessings over my life.

To my parents, Henry & Lamona. Thank you for serving as both my biological and spiritual parents, planting the seed of God's Word in my heart that others may water. You were my first models of what following Christ looked like and continue to disciple me to this day. And to my brother Shareef – the best big brother in the world!

To my childhood church family, Mt. Sinai. Thanks to all who poured the truth of God's Word into my heart and continued to build on the foundation laid by my parents. To my Sunday School, VBS and Bible Study teachers Ms. Morgan, Ms. Davis, Ms. Jamison, Rev. Cooley, Lee-Lee, Tony and others. To the Junior Usher Board, who provided me the first opportunity to serve - Eddie, Jackie, Curtis, Mario, Carl, and others.

To my college church family, New United. Thanks for being the first to expose me to the Inductive Bible Study method. You are a church family that is dear to my heart, acknowledging my gift of teaching as a teen and even allowing me to teach adult classes. All the best to the crew: Jeff, Yolanda, Levasia, and Melody.

To my adult church family, EBC. Thanks to Pastor Oliver and Dr. Smith for your outstanding leadership and consistently challenging me to stretch further. Special thanks to my co-laborers in the Greenhouse youth ministry.

CONTENTS

INTRODUCTION

Welcome to Inductive Bible Study!

If you have never studied the Bible before, or if you have been a follower of Jesus for some time but desire to understand more of the "deep and hidden things" God promises He will reveal for those who read and study His Word (Dan. 2:22), this book is for you. By following a few simple steps, and committing to learn the how of Inductive Bible Study, you will come to a more intimate relationship with God. In addition, by using this easy to follow guide you will learn how to accurately interpret and apply God's Word, thereby experiencing its life transforming power!

The first four chapters of the book will walk you through the steps to Inductive Bible Study. Then, Chapter 5 will talk about the importance of memorizing and meditating on Scripture. Chapter 6 includes the practical—organizing everything you will need for Inductive Bible Study. Chapter 7 includes invaluable information on how to complete Greek and Hebrew word studies. Finally, a number of appendices are included in the back of the book on important topics related to interpreting the Bible, such as Typology and Interpreting Prophecy.

Inductive Bible Study is not hard! But it does take time and a desire to learn. The techniques laid out in *Stop Reading, Start Studying: Inductive Bible Study Method Explained* will change the way you read, study and interpret the Bible, and ultimately, change your life.

You will never be the same again. You will be *transformed.*

CHAPTER 1

WATER FROM THE WELL

*"Everyone who drinks of this water will thirst again; but whoever drinks of the water that I will give him shall never thirst; but the water that I will give him will become in him a well of water springing up to eternal life." – **John 4:13–14***

M any people long to have a deeper relationship with God, but aren't sure what steps to take to make that happen. Christians who have participated in Bible Studies for many years may still feel intimidated by their Bibles, lost at how to find certain books or verses. Newer followers of Jesus may simply not know where to begin. There are hundreds of different ways to study the Bible, but many have come to learn and love the Inductive Bible Study method.

It's not about what book of the Bible you study, how long you study a certain passage or where you study your Bible. It's about knowing who God is. It is about relationship. A relationship with God is not about laws, customs, or man-made rules. Though these things may make a person look "spiritual" on the outside, they are unproductive when it comes to achieving a real knowledge of God.

In his book *Transformed by the Renewing of Your Mind* (Jubilee Publishing, 2003) Robert Shirock compares Bible Study to a computer program. He writes that it is not good enough to have the latest software program collecting dust on the top of a shelf; the program must be loaded onto your computer and ready to run. "In the same way," he writes, "it is not enough to have thoughts and ideas about the Bible sitting on a shelf. God's thoughts will not transform your life until those thoughts are loaded on the computer of your mind and ready to run in the daily course of life." [45]

The very Word of God needs to form in your mind, and there is no shortcut to achieving that result. Knowing *about* God is not enough. You've got to know *God*, and who He is—His character, heart and will—and the only way to accomplish this is by studying the Bible.

*"O God, You are my God; I shall seek You earnestly; My soul thirsts for You, my flesh yearns for You, In a dry and weary land where there is no water." – **Psalm 63:1***

In your journey towards a deeper understanding of God through Inductive Bible Study, the Bible will be your primary source. The Bible says the Word of God is the "water" that washes and cleanses (John 17:17; Eph. 5:26), the only thing that can renew your mind. Jesus affirmed this, teaching His disciples, "You are already clean *because of the word* I have spoken to you" (John 15:3, emphasis added). The Word of Christ dwelling within men and women is what purifies.

It is through the Bible that the God of the universe will speak directly to you, His beloved creation. Every word in your Bible is living and active and given by God for your benefit and to bring you into a more intimate relationship with Him. The apostle Paul wrote:

"All Scripture is inspired by God and profitable for teaching, for reproof, for correction, for training in righteousness."
– 2 Timothy 3:16, emphasis added

Notice Paul didn't say, "some Scripture," or "the parts of the Bible that are easy to understand." He said *all Scripture* is inspired by God to be used for teaching, reproof and correction. Teaching, reproof and correction refine the child of God, transforming them towards holiness. Paul also wrote that Scripture is to be used for training in righteousness. Why? The answer is found in the very next verse:

*"...so that the man of God may be adequate, equipped for every good work." – **2 Timothy 3:17***

There is work to be done as a believer, and God will not leave you ill equipped. The Word of God will prepare you for the calling God has on your life. You don't need anything else. There are many good commentaries, lexicons, books and articles about the Word of God. However, the key to successful Inductive Bible Study is the careful and prayerful observance of the actual Word of God, and an invitation for the Holy Spirit to be your teacher and "tell you great and mighty things, which you do not know" (Jer. 33:3).

> *"Never let good books take the place of the Bible. Drink from the Well, not from the streams that flow from the Well."*
> — *Amy Carmichael*

Studying the Word of God initiates a process in the human soul, out of which faith develops. It nourishes, satisfies a thirst that only God can quench, heals both physically and mentally, gives victory over sin and Satan, and cleanses. In a nutshell, the Word of God transforms the spiritually dead person to one who is alive in Christ and conforms them to the image of the invisible God (Rom. 8:29).

INDUCTIVE BIBLE STUDY

Inductive Bible Study is much more than a way to learn more facts about the Bible; the ultimate purpose of Inductive Bible Study is life transformation—to become more like Jesus.

Instead of studying resources *about* the Bible, inductive study places chief significance upon the Bible itself. To receive the greatest benefit, you will need to be willing to lay aside preconceived philosophies, study notes, sermon tapes, commentaries and even trite sayings and approach the Bible as if you are approaching it as a new believer for the first time.

According to Peter, the Scriptures alone are more than enough to radically change your life. Reminding Christians of the basics of the faith, Peter writes:

> *"His divine power has granted to us* everything *pertaining to life and godliness, through the true knowledge of Him who called us by His own glory and excellence. For by these He has granted to us His precious and magnificent promises, so that by them you may become partakers of the divine nature, having escaped the corruption that is in the world by lust."*
> **– 2 Peter 1:3–4, emphasis added**

God's Word contains everything you need to know about life and godliness through the knowledge of Him—and this knowledge of God can only be found in His Word. It follows that to learn more about God, you must study the Bible.

Your life will be directed by what you focus most of your time and attention on, what you "delight in." Ezra, a scribe and high priest who lived in ancient Babylon during the Jewish exile, understood the importance of studying God's Word: "For Ezra had set his heart to study the law of the LORD and to practice it, and to teach His statutes and ordinances in Israel" (Ezra 7:10). The psalmist declared that studying the Scriptures results in a fruitful life of blessing:

> *"But his delight is in the law of the Lord, And in His law he meditates day and night. He will be like a tree firmly planted by streams of water, Which yields its fruit in its season And its leaf does not wither; And in whatever he does, he prospers."*
> **– Psalm 1:1–3**

The Bible you hold in your hand contains precious promises of blessing for anyone willing to study it and walk in obedience to its commands. These are those whom Peter calls "partakers of the divine nature" (2 Pet. 1:4). Not one single word of God is void of power; every single "jot and tittle" (Matt. 5:18 KJV) is pregnant with life and revelation of God and His Messiah, Jesus Christ. [39]

Are you ready to be radically transformed by the Word of God? Are you ready to be changed forever by what the writer of Hebrews calls, "...living and active, sharper than any two-edged sword, piercing to the division of soul and of spirit, of joints and of marrow, and discerning the thoughts and intentions of the heart" (Heb. 4:12 ESV)? [37]

Begin with a commitment to read and study your Bible as if God Himself is speaking directly to you...*because He is.*

WHAT IS INDUCTIVE BIBLE STUDY?

B efore you begin learning how to study inductively, it's important to understand some basics. What exactly is Inductive Bible Study?

The word "inductive" means, "To use logical induction and reasoning by examining the particulars, facts, and essence of a text—such as context and word meanings—before making any conclusions." [6]

Inductive Bible Study is thus an approach to God's Word that progresses from a general synopsis to specifics. Then, inductive *reasoning* is applied—the attempt to use information about a specific situation to draw a conclusion. Inductive Bible Study helps people find the central truth of a passage on their own, and build that truth into their life. Noted Inductive Bible Study teacher Kay Arthur has this to say about studying inductively:

*"Inductive Bible study draws you into personal interaction with the Scripture and thus with the God of the Scriptures so that your beliefs are based on a prayerful understanding and legitimate interpretation of Scripture—truth that transforms you when you live by it." – **Kay Arthur**[33]*

THREE BASIC STEPS

There are three basic steps foundational for Inductive Bible Study: *Observation, Interpretation, and Application.* These three steps, once understood and applied, will bring tremendous breakthrough in your ability to understand the Word of God.

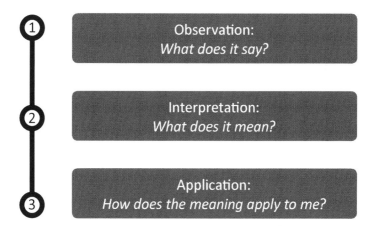

1. Observation:
What does it say?

2. Interpretation:
What does it mean?

3. Application:
How does the meaning apply to me?

We will delve deeper into each of these three steps in later chapters. For now, please tuck away the importance of asking questions when studying Scripture. Notice that each of the above steps asks a question. John Piper wrote, "One of the great problems in Bible

"Studying the Bible inductively will help transform your life to be more like Christ."

reading is that we move our eyes over the words and come to the end of a column and don't know what we've read; we don't feel our minds or spirits expanded because we saw nothing fresh. It was purely mechanical. There was no discovery, no life, and no breakthroughs to new insight. One of the best ways to change that is to train yourself *to ask questions of the text*" (emphasis added).

Asking these three basic questions—What does it say? What does the text mean? How does that meaning apply to me?—are the crux of Inductive Bible Study.

WHY INDUCTIVE BIBLE STUDY?

P eople learn more when they are actively involved in the learning process, according to research. They remember ten percent of what they read, twenty percent of what they hear, and thirty percent of what they watch. They will remember fifty percent of what they hear and watch combined.

However, when what is heard and watched is written out, that number jumps to seventy percent! And when everything learned is then *applied*, ninety percent is retained.

Inductive Bible Study is effective because it combines each of these things: reading, hearing, watching and applying the Word of God.

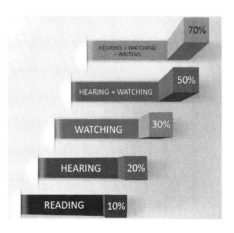

As previously stated, the Scriptures are the primary source with Inductive Bible Study. As a result, the learner becomes less dependent on secondary resources and more receptive to and dependent on the Holy Spirit. When truth is discovered, there is more joy because the discovery hasn't come from someone else retelling an insight; it comes from the relationship between the student and God as his or her teacher, through the Word.

Consider Job's words regarding his relationship with God:

"I have not departed from the command of His lips; I have treasured the words of His mouth more than my necessary food." – Job 23:12

Job was an upright, God-fearing man known for turning from evil. The secret to Job's consistently holy life was his relationship with God. Job knew God's voice. God's words were priceless treasures for Job, and they transformed him. May you come to such a deeper understanding of the Lord and His Word, like the prophet Job, that you hunger and thirst for it more than anything in life! May the Word of God abide in you, too, speak to you and transform you as you study.

IS INDUCTIVE BIBLE STUDY BIBLICAL?

Y ou may be wondering, "Who invented Inductive Bible Study? Did anyone in the Bible study this way? Is it *biblical*?

In the book of Acts, Paul makes a statement that is often overlooked. The author of Acts, Luke, writes that the Jews had become jealous and stirred up discord in Thessalonica. This resulted in the church sending Paul and Silas away during the night to a town known as Berea.

When Paul and Silas arrived, they immediately went to the Jewish synagogue. Luke writes, "The people of Berea were more open-minded than those in Thessalonica, and they listened eagerly to

> *"Be diligent to present yourself approved to God as a workman who does not need to be ashamed, accurately handling the word of truth."*
> **– 2 Timothy 2:15**

Paul's message. They searched the Scriptures day after day to check up on Paul and Silas, to see if they were really teaching the truth" (Acts 17:10–12 NLT). [43]

The Bereans, a people from the northern part of ancient Greece, were studying inductively! Notice they did not compare Paul's words with a commentary, a radio podcast or a blog posting. They received the word "eagerly," and then "searched the Scriptures" for themselves. "Searched" or "examined" comes from the Greek word *anakrino*, meaning, "to judge up and down." Being open-minded (or "noble-minded" in the NIV)[42] conveys a willingness to learn and evaluate something fairly.

Picture the Bereans scrutinizing those ancient Hebrew scrolls, eyes scanning the parchment by the light of an oil lamp, looking intently for truth. From the Scriptures and the leading of the Holy Spirit, they then formed a verdict regarding Paul's message. The Bereans made use of a divine timeless principle: personal study of the Scriptures will shed light on any secondary resource.

> *"It is not commentaries, councils or creeds that should mould our Christian beliefs, however valuable some of them may be, but the Word of God."*
> **– Brian Edwards**

TWO PREREQUISITES

"I study my Bible as I gather apples. First, I shake the whole tree that the ripest might fall. Then I shake each limb, and when I have shaken each limb, I shake each branch and every

twig. Then I look under every leaf. I shake the Bible as a whole, like shaking the whole tree. Then I shake every limb— study book after book. Then I shake every branch, giving attention to the chapters when they do not break the sense. Then I shake every twig, or a careful study of the paragraphs and sentences and words and their meanings."

– Martin Luther

Before committing to study your Bible inductively, there a couple of things you must be willing to do.

First, you must be prepared to slow down. This current generation is high-strung, neurotic, and impatient, ensnared by instant messaging, instant credit, instant oatmeal…instant *everything*. Without realizing it, most people have slid into the "now" trap. Nowadays you can even order and pay for your Starbucks coffee from your hand-held device; that coffee will be ready the second you walk in the store and be in your hand without your having to say "hello" to anyone!

This attitude will simply not work with Inductive Bible Study. Inductive Bible Study takes time, and should always begin with significant prayer. Slow down. Find a quiet place to study, and take a big breath. Invite the Holy Spirit to join you before you even open your Bible. Then ask God to remove the veils off of your eyes so you might see spiritual truth in what you are about to study (Ps. 119:18). He promises He will "…give you the treasures of darkness, And hidden wealth of secret places, So that you may know that it is I, The Lord, the God of Israel, who calls you by your name" (Isa. 45:3).

God is waiting to reveal deep and hidden things to you so that you will know Him more intimately. How profound! Knowing this, will you commit to studying your Bible slowly, and discipline yourself to be patient?

> *"For when your patience is finally in full bloom, then you will be ready for anything, strong in character."*
> **– James 1:4b (TLB)[48]**

Then, before you read one line out of your Bible, set aside any preconceived biases. Without realizing it, these fixed ideas can actually keep you from seeing truth in Scripture. Often, doctrines learned from the first teacher a person encounters after putting their faith in Christ subconsciously become the standard by which they interpret Scripture. Or, whatever a pastor teaches from the pulpit is regarded as truth. Unfortunately, their doctrine may not always be sound.

The prophet Isaiah wrote, "'For My thoughts are not your thoughts, Nor are your ways My ways,' declares the Lord" (Isa. 55:8). Commit to carefully observe what the passage says, regardless of prior education, teaching, or experience. God, whose ways are higher than any one person's (no matter how educated they may be), will be your most excellent teacher. And if your preconceived ideas are correct, they will stand as you diligently study the Scriptures.

BENEFITS OF STUDYING INDUCTIVELY

It is important to re-state that studying inductively is far more than acquiring piles of knowledge. The Bible says the "fear of the LORD" is the foundation of wisdom, and "the knowledge of the Holy One is understanding" (Prov. 9:10). Worldly wisdom might be well reasoned and seem effective on the surface, but the formula won't work with God. This kind of wisdom, based on puffed up knowledge, is foolishness in God's eyes (1 Cor. 3:19). Godly wisdom is living in, through, and from a relationship with Christ.

God wants a deeper dependence on, a richer relationship with, and a more authentic experience of Himself for you.

Studying inductively will help you learn to carefully observe the Scriptures. In doing you will be enabled to accurately handle the word of truth (2 Tim. 2:15). You will be better equipped to interpret God's Word on your own and apply it to your personal life.

You will learn to study independent of commentaries, devotionals or pastor's sermons. You won't need powerful motivational Christian conferences to get you excited about a passage in the Bible! Good and godly teachers of the Word are necessary and a gift from the Lord, but they should not become a substitute for studying the Bible.

As you become more comfortable with Inductive Bible Study, your ability to see differences in interpretations will be strengthened; as a result, when you reference secondary resources, you will be able to discern which ones represent a more accurate interpretation...and which ones *don't*.

"They who would grow in grace must be inquisitive."

– Matthew Henry

Ultimately, your knowledge of God and His ways will increase, and you will mature "in the grace and knowledge of our Lord and Savior Jesus Christ" (2 Pet. 3:18). Your relationship with God will grow, and you will be transformed.

CHAPTER 2

OBSERVATION: WHAT DOES IT SAY?

*"The goal of observation is to enable one to become saturated with the particulars of a passage so that one is thoroughly conscious of the object being observed." – **Robert Traina**[49]*

The Power of God's Word

The Bible is unlike anything you will ever read, and it provides wisdom you will never find in any other book. It is unique in its authorship, authority, accuracy, adequacy and its agenda. The Word of God is a lamp in the darkness (Ps. 119:105), and its testimony is "righteous forever" (Ps. 119:144). The Holy Spirit has anointed every word in the Bible, and it has the power to transform you. However, you must be willing to engage and wrestle with those words for transformation to happen.

The Bible addresses every single need a person will ever have. It is eternal; the things of this world will pass away, but Scripture says the Word of God will remain forever (1 Pet. 1:23–25). The Bible nourishes, and it reveals. It admonishes, exhorts and comforts (1 Pet. 2:2). Above all, God's instruction found within the pages of Scripture is the only thing that has the power to save and thus bring peace (Isa. 55:11; John 6:63; Heb. 4:12).

No book written by man has knowledge directly inspired by God Himself. It is God's blueprint for life, His plan set forth before the beginning of time culminating in the rule and reign of Jesus Christ on earth. It is available for anyone willing to dive in and commit to the journey. Are you ready? Let's begin!

Observation

The first and most important step in Inductive Bible Study is *observation*. Observation describes "the act of taking notice, fixing the mind upon, and beholding with attention, with the goal of discovering what the text says."[20] Observation attempts to discover what the passage says.

Start with the proper approach: prayer. Ask God to open your eyes, "that [you] may behold Wonderful things from [His] law" (Ps. 119:18). Communication with God is often left pushed aside;

however, it is essential to approach the Word of God with the right heart and mindset. Next, prepare to take notes as you study.

In this first step, you will look at what the author said and ask yourself questions to establish what is going on.

Observation involves examining the obvious. Dr. H. T. Kuist defines observation as, "the art of seeing things as they really are." Facts about people, places and events are pretty easy to distinguish in biblical writing because the writers tend to repeat these facts. Let the text speak for itself. Don't try to read anything into a passage of Scripture, or attempt to "spiritualize" it. Also, read the text devotionally, with a "heart that wants to see what God is saying to you."[33]

> *How many books have you ever read where you had the benefit of the author's presence to help you discern his original intent?*
> *– Anonymous*

Your main goal for this first step is to try and establish the author's original intent...not your intent, your pastor's intent or your Bible study leader's intent. What was the author trying to communicate to his readers or listeners?

Next, to discover the author's original intent, you must establish the correct context.

ESTABLISH CONTEXT

Establishing context will lay the foundation for accurate interpretation. Context means, "That which goes with the text." It is the setting in which a passage occurs. Thus, it's important to examine those verses immediately before and after the passage you are studying. Consider also the book in which the passage appears, as well as other books by the same author. Doing so will help determine how the passage fits into the overall message of the entire Bible.

To establish context, read, re-read and read again the text you hope to interpret. Carefully observe the text for repeated facts and truths. First, read the passage and look for obvious things. People, places, and events are usually easy to identify. In the epistles (such as Galatians, 1 & 2 Corinthians or 1 & 2 Timothy), start by observing facts about the author and the letter's recipients. By starting with the obvious, things within a book that are not as easy to see or understand or are confusing will eventually become clearer.

Next, determine any other helpful background. Who is the author? What is the setting of the text (or book)? Is there a clear purpose for writing? To whom is the author writing?

Consider also the cultural setting of the text. The Bible was originally written within many different cultural backgrounds, which will affect how you understand the passage. For example, Paul asked the question in 1 Corinthians 11:13: "Is it proper for a woman to pray to God with her head uncovered?" Quick research will reveal that in ancient Judaism, women covered their heads not only for prayer but whenever they were outside of their homes. Knowing this simple fact will help when trying to figure out later on why Paul was asking this question!

Contemplate, too, the genre of the book you are studying (see Appendix C for more on genre). The Bible contains poetry, wise sayings, history, letters (epistles), prophetic writings, and apocalyptic (prophetic) literature. Understanding genre will affect how you later interpret a passage. Finally, note the historical background. What was going on historically at the time this passage or book was written? Robert Shirock states, "A thorough background study is an essential element in the mastery of a Bible book. The basic goal is to get knee-deep in the historical setting."[45]

Why is it so important to establish context? Because, in Inductive Bible Study, context is king—context often drives the meaning of a phrase. You won't be able to interpret any text accurately without first understanding the context.

> *"From the standpoint of the Bible as literature, the simplest error of reading is the failure to consider the immediate context of the verse or passage in question. The literature of the cults is filled with illustrations of this basic mistake."*
> **– James Sire, Scripture Twisting: 20 Ways the Cults Misread the Bible**[46]

ACTIVE V. PASSIVE READING

Many people find it hard to "pay attention" while reading Scripture. The best way to solve this problem is to read actively, verses passively. Active reading asks questions; it requires you to be active in your mind as you read the Bible! Be encouraged. This is not natural for most people! You must train yourself to do it.

One of the best ways to train yourself to think about what you are reading is to write your thoughts as they come to mind while reading. This process will help you sustain a sequence of questions and answers long enough to come to conclusions.

The first step to doing this is to identify and mark *key words*.

IDENTIFY AND MARK KEY WORDS

Your car keys unlock the door allowing you to enter the vehicle and also allow you to drive. If you misplace them, you can't get from point A to B! This is what "key words or phrases" do. They function as the keys to your "car" to help you unlock the meaning of what you are studying. Then, they move you from "A to B", from observation to interpretation. [20]

Key words are usually easy to identify because they are repeated. They may include pronouns, synonyms, or closely related phrases. They can be key to just one paragraph, or sometimes the entire chapter or book.

Color-coding. Mark these phrases in your Bible by placing a colored symbol over the key word or phrase. This will identify the word quickly, and you will begin to get a sense of its relationship to the section as a whole. (For more information on how to mark key words and phrases, see *Chapter 6: Getting Organized*)

If you are the creative sort, you can purchase color pencils and draw markings on the pages of your Bible. Otherwise, the free Inductive Bible Study app comes pre-stocked with hundreds of suggested colors and symbols for commonly repeated words or phrases in the Bible. To view a comprehensive listing, visit http://InductiveBibleStudyApp.com/bookextras.

Recall in Chapter 1 that people remember fifty percent of what they read, hear and see. Marking helps you take ownership of the Scripture, and they will help you remember the text. They will allow you to scan quickly the page and identify the key words that the author purposefully emphasized in a given passage.

Each encounter with a key word should encourage a question such as: Why is this word used in this sentence or passage? How does it impact the author's flow of thought? To whom was this word intended? These types of questions are called *The Big 6 Questions.*

Investigative reporters interrogate, or examine; they ask formal and methodical questions. As you train yourself to examine the text, meaning will be revealed to you as the Holy Spirit illuminates Scripture.

Like a journalist, you must learn to ask what we are calling the "Big 6" Questions: *Who, What, Why, Where, When,* and *How?*

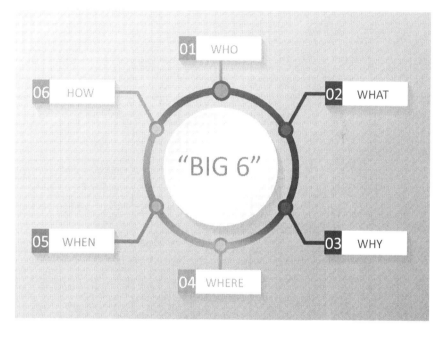

1. **Who** is speaking? To whom and about whom is this person speaking? Who wrote the passage? Who are the main characters? Who else is mentioned in the book?

2. **What** is the author doing? What are the main events? What are the circumstances? What are the main ideas? What is the historical or cultural setting (as determined from the text)? What is the genre of the passage? What is the theme of the chapter or book?

3. **Why** was this written? Why is a particular thing said? Why is he/she in a certain place?

4. **Where** did (or will) this happen? Where was this book/ passage written or said? Where did the main events of the passage take place?

5. **When** was this written (on the Biblical history timeline)? When was this passage written the author's life? When did (or will) this happen? When did the author say/do it?

6. **How** will (or did) something happen? How is the truth illustrated? How did the passage/message/book/letter affect people?

Don't be frustrated if you are not able to answer every one of the "Big 6" Questions every time; this is ok and common. Asking these questions will force you to slow down and counteract the tendency to read through a passage hastily. You'll begin to realize your heart and mind are far more engaged with Scripture than before!

Asking these questions will allow you to pull out facts and examine the context through the nature of Scripture. Doing so will help you avoid presumptions and fallacies that lead to false teaching. As we've said, the Word of God speaks for itself.

You will start to acquire insights into the Word of God that you could not have discovered from a quick surface reading, and you will begin to experience the joy of self-discovery.

CHAPTER AND VERSE DIVISIONS

Another method of observation is to make chapter and verse divisions. Chapters and verses were actually not part of the Bible as it was originally written! Many "books" are actually letters written to churches. Over the ages, translators have added in these divisions but sometimes they can do more to trip you up than to help.

One effective method of Inductive Bible Study is to survey the entire book, seeking the big picture, and then break it up into chapters and paragraphs as *you* see fit. This will help you to see more easily the significance of the book as a whole.

IDENTIFY THE CENTRAL THEME

A t this point, you should be able to identify the theme of the chapter or book. The theme will tend to center on a main person, event, teaching or subject; it will often be revealed in your list of key words, and by an additional reading of the text. Hopefully, the theme is obvious. Ask yourself: *What seems to be the central focus of the book or the chapter of the book?* See if you can write it in a short sentence.

Whenever a person begins to approach a book, a chapter or a section, the central theme or subject must be grasped and this comes only by reading it over and over again until the central theme stands out as the sun illuminating the rest of the material." – **Pastor Xavior Reis, Calvary Chapel Pasadena**

CONNECTING WORDS AND PHRASES

L ook also for connecting words and phrases. Connecting words and phrases join clauses, passages, paragraphs, and chapters together. Though they may seem insignificant, they are powerful words that connect the writer's train of thought into a unified whole. These are common words, but once you learn to watch for them as you study inductively, they will illuminate the meaning of a passage, paragraph or chapter. Let's examine types of connecting words for a moment.

Terms of Conclusion

A term of conclusion identifies a logical consequence or conclusion or summarizes a preceding argument. Terms of conclusion are words and phrases like *Therefore, So, For this reason,* and *So then.*

An example of a term of conclusion in the Bible is, "How much more valuable then is a man than a sheep! **So then**, it is lawful to do good on the Sabbath" (Matt. 12:12).

Terms of Explanation

Terms of explanation introduce the reason for something, making it plain or understandable. These words give reasons why something is true or why something occurred, or give additional information. Sometimes they express cause or give additional information. Terms of conclusion are words like *For* and *Because.*

An example of a term of explanation is used twice in Romans 1:16 by Paul: "**For** I am not ashamed of the gospel, **for** it is the power of God for salvation to everyone who believes, to the Jew first and also to the Greek."

Terms of Purpose

Terms of purpose indicate the intended or end goal of an idea or action, or the effect, aim, design or consequence of something. They provide the reason something is done. Terms of purpose are words or phrases such as *So that, In order that* (or *In order to*) and *That.*

Three examples in Scripture of terms of purpose can be found in Exodus 20:20 alone: "Do not be afraid; for God has come **in order to** test you, and **in order that** the fear of Him may remain with you, **so that** you may not sin."

When observing Scripture and one of these connecting words or phrases appears, immediately ask yourself the Big 6 Questions: *Who, What, Why, Where, When, and How?* You'll be surprised at how much insight you will receive!

OTHER THINGS TO LOOK FOR

I n addition to connecting words and phrases, be on the lookout for terms of contrast. They will usually be evident by the words or phrases *But, But rather, However, In spite of, Instead of, Nevertheless, On the other hand,* and *Yet.* John Phillips rightly said, "Oh, those revealing *'buts'* of the Bible. They are small hinges on which great truths and destinies swing." Don't pass over these words too quickly! You may miss something profound.

Make note of geographic locations, contrasts, expressions of time and figurative language. These are additional keys that may bring a deeper understanding to a particular passage.

We will show you how to do all of this in *Chapter 6: Getting Organized.* Hold tight!

ADDITIONAL QUESTIONING

A sking questions is an art to be learned. The following are additional questions that could be asked when observing a text:

- Does this passage discuss the life, work, teaching and presence of Jesus Christ?

- What is the mood of the passage? Rejoicing? Sorrow?

- What literary form (genre) does the text have?

- How does the passage fit into Israel's history?

- Are there any promises being stated?

- Is there a lesson being taught?

- Is the passage teaching anything about God's character?

- Are there any commands?

- Are there any contrasts?

- Is there a prophecy in the passage? Is the book written by a prophet?

- Are there any repeated words or phrases?

- Is any Old Testament prophecy or Scripture being cited in the New Testament passage you are reading?

- Is there a problem and solution?

- Does this passage connect to other books or passages of the Bible?

This list is certainly not exhaustive but gives you an idea of the many questions you can ask when observing your text. Once you've completed the observation step, you will be ready to move on to the second step: *Interpretation.*

CHAPTER 3

INTERPRETATION: WHAT DOES IT MEAN?

"Concerning this salvation, the prophets, who spoke of the grace that was to come to you, searched intently and with the greatest care, *trying to find out the time and circumstances to which the Spirit of Christ in them was pointing when he predicted the sufferings of the Messiah and the glories that would follow."* – *1 Peter 1:10-12, NIV, emphasis added*

G. Campbell Morgan, a well-known British pastor and evangelist, told the humorous story of a man who studied his Bible haphazardly, like flipping a coin. Whatever he opened his Bible to at that moment he took as God's Word to him.

Once when he followed that method the man came up with, "Judas went out and hanged himself" (Matt. 27:5 KJV). Finding these words unhelpful, he did it again and this time he landed on, "Go, and do thou likewise" (Luke 10:37 KJV). In desperation, he tried once more and this time the words that jumped at him were, "That thou doest, do quickly" (John 13:27 KJV).[19]

Although comical, there is a serious lesson to be learned. The Bible should not be approached in a mystical, superstitious or haphazard way. Peter exhorts followers of Jesus to strive to "rightly [divide] the word of truth" (2 Tim. 2:15 KJV). It does not take a seminary degree to be able to read and interpret Scripture accurately; however, it must be done correctly and with reverence. God said through the prophet Isaiah, "But to this one I will look, To him who is humble and contrite of spirit, and who trembles at My word" (Isa. 66:2).

What is Interpretation?

Webster's Dictionary defines interpretation as explaining or telling the meaning of something and presenting it in understandable terms. Biblical interpretation (hermeneutics) seeks to walk in the author's shoes with the ultimate goal being able to understand or explain their original intent. Ultimately, it is God's intent, expressed through human writers inspired by the Holy Spirit:

"But know this first of all, that no prophecy of Scripture is a matter of one's own interpretation, for no prophecy was ever made by an act of human will, but men moved by the Holy Spirit *spoke from God."*
– 2 Peter 1:20–21, emphasis added

Dr. Howard Hendricks compared interpretation to a building: "In observation we excavate. In interpretation we erect." A building's stability is determined by its foundation. The more secure the foundation, the more dependable the structure. In the same way, interpretation will come more readily and be more secure when the observation process has been thoroughly completed. When approached correctly, interpretation becomes a strong bridge between observation and application.

May you (as the prophets did) search the Scriptures intently and "with the greatest care" to arrive at meaning that is sound, and application that is effective.

GENERAL PRINCIPLES OF INTERPRETATION

S ometimes it will be tempting to try and force the Scriptures to agree with whatever you want the passage to say; this is a misleading and risky trap.

John MacArthur gives this example of a misinterpretation of Matthew 18:12–20:

"How many times have you heard somebody say this in a prayer meeting: 'Where two or three are gathered together in my name, there am I in the midst of them. Friends, two or three of us are here, so the Lord is here.' Do you want to know something? If I'm there alone, the Lord is there! That verse has nothing to do with a prayer meeting. If you study the context and the grammar, you find that out. What it's saying is that when you discipline somebody, when you put somebody out of the church, and his sin has been confirmed by two or three witnesses, Christ said that He is in their midst."

How important it is to observe Scripture well, and then properly interpret it!

Misinterpretation is far too common among students of the Bible. How can this be avoided? Applying the following simple interpretive principles will help you guard against interpreting the Bible incorrectly.

1. Base Your Interpretation on the Author's Original Intent

Many times people will base interpretation on popular accord, gut feelings, powerful or persuasive arguments, or even what other respected teachers and scholars have taught.

However, interpretation must be based on the author's intended meaning, not the reader's opinion or anyone else's. The context the author wrote in, as well as the history, grammar, culture, literary form, and conventions the author was working in must be considered. It has been some 2000 years since many of those authors documented God's Word, and their world was very different than ours! One of the great leaders of the Reformation in Switzerland, Ulrich Zwingli says interpreting without considering what the author intended is like "breaking off a flower from its roots."

To understand the importance of context in interpretation, consider the sentence, "It was a ball." What exactly does this phrase mean?

The answer depends on the context! Consider the following:

A The baseball umpire saw the pitch drift to the outside and said, "It was a ball."

B We went to the dance last night; it was so formal, "it was a ball."

C As I was walking along the golf course, I spotted something small and white in the tall grass. "It was a ball."

D I had so much fun at the game night. "It was a ball."

In each sentence above, "ball" means something different. Context is necessary to determine the true meaning. Try to guard against interpreting a text in isolation from the context it was written in. You will find it helpful when interpreting Scripture to give the most weight to the nearest context.

Some good questions to help you discover cultural and historical context may include:

- What were the times like when this passage was written?

- What was the attitude toward Christianity when this was written?

- When is this taking place?

- What else was taking place in the world at this time?

- What did the specific passage mean to the people to whom it was spoken or written?

- What were some of the social and political influences on the writer and on those to whom he was writing?

2. Read and Interpret the Bible Literally

In addition to interpreting Scripture based on the author's original intent, hold to the normal literal meaning of the text. Constantly searching for some deeper spiritual meaning is guaranteed to take you off-track. There are of course spiritual aspects to many passages; however, the authors normally make this clear.

"If the literal meaning of any word or expression makes good sense in its connections, it is literal; but if the literal meaning does not make good sense, it is figurative. Since the literal is the most usual signification of a word, and, therefore, occurs

*much more frequently than the figurative, any term should be regarded as literal until there is good reason for a different understanding." – **Clinton Lockhart, Principles of Interpretation**[40]*

The best argument for taking the Bible literally is because Jesus Himself did. When the Scribes and Pharisees demanded Jesus perform a sign to prove who He said he was, Jesus referred to a familiar text in the Hebrew Scriptures that those Scribes and Pharisees knew well:

*"An evil and adulterous generation craves for a sign; and yet no sign will be given to it but the sign of Jonah the prophet; for just as Jonah was three days and three nights in the belly of the sea monster, so will the Son of Man be three days and three nights in the heart of the earth." – **Matthew 12:39-40***

Did Jesus use this example of Jonah allegorically? Absolutely not! He referred to Jonah's literal time in the belly of the great fish to foretell how long He would be in the grave. Jesus interpreted the Scriptures literally.

And so should we.

3. Compare Scripture with Scripture

Warren Wiersbe writes, "We must never divorce one part of Scripture from another, but we must always "compare spiritual things with spiritual.'"

This means interpretation of a passage should never be done in isolation to the rest of the Bible. At the very minimum, examine the paragraph in which the passage is embedded. Then read the passage within the context of the chapter, and then in light of the book as a whole. Cross-reference other passages that may shed light on the one you are studying. This is crucial to understanding the correct meaning of a passage. Why? Evangelical pastor and author Rick Warren gives this reason:

"The Bible is its own best commentary. Scripture interprets Scripture. Practice this principle by getting a Bible with cross-references in the margin. By looking up other cross references, you'll get a much bigger and clearer picture of what God has said in all of his Word, not just that one context."
– Rick Warren

Scripture never contradicts itself. If your interpretation differs from truth found in another passage, you can be sure you have arrived at an inaccurate understanding. Though your interpretation may be wrong, God's interpretation never is...He always agrees with Himself! One piece of Scripture may be the "key" that unlocks another piece of Scripture:

*"Scripture is the best interpreter of Scripture. The locks of Scripture are only to be opened with the keys of Scripture; and there is no lock in the whole Bible, which God meant us to open, without a key to fit it somewhere in the Bible, and we are to search for it until we find it." – **C. H. Spurgeon***

4. Seek External Resources

Once you've looked at the context the author wrote in and compared Scripture with Scripture, you can then move on to seek the interpretation of learned theologians. The first tool every student of the Bible should obtain is a good study Bible with notes that explain historical and cultural background information. These will prove invaluable in the interpretive process. Second, he or she should have access to a variety of evangelical commentaries. In this day, there are many wonderful commentaries that can be easily accessed on the Internet.

Concordances, expository dictionaries, and encyclopedias may also be helpful in your studies. Concordances are alphabetical lists of biblical words that reference everywhere these words occur in specific translations of the Bible. Expository dictionaries provide more holistic definitions, names and verse references for biblical words. Biblical encyclopedias contain articles and definitions for words and terms in the Bible and also include historical context and verse references. Each of these will be a valuable resource.

5. Identify Figures of Speech and Parables in Historical Context

Though we are to interpret Scripture from a literal perspective, the Bible is also full of metaphorical language, figures of speech and stories. When it is clear the author is using one of these literary techniques, interpret what appears to be metaphorical against historical data to see if the meaning was different in the time it was written.

Figures of speech such as similes, metaphors, hyperbole and personification increase the power of a word or the force of an expression. Look at Isaiah 55:12b that reads, "The mountains and the hills will break forth into shouts of joy before you, And all the trees of the field will clap their hands." Mountains do not shout, and trees do not clap! This is called personification—when physical, inanimate objects are given human characteristics to bring attention to the point being made.

Or take for example the metaphorical story of the vine and the branches in John 15. The New American Standard Bible (NASB) version says that God "takes away" any branch that does not bear fruit in John 15:2. In English, it would seem that God is removing branches. However, in the original Greek the word for "takes away" is *meno* that describes the 'lifting' of a branch away from the ground. Agricultural practices in the ancient Middle East involved placing a vine in a position where it would receive more sun and thrive better. Insight like this is critical to correct interpretation.

"God spoke to us that we might know truth. Therefore, take the Word of God at face value—in its natural, normal sense. Look first for the clear teaching of Scripture, not a hidden meaning. Understand and recognize figures of speech and interpret them accordingly."
– Kay Arthur, How to Study Your Bible[33]

Don't settle for a figure of speech unless it is clearly indicated as such. Words or phrases should be understood in a literal sense unless the resulting sense involves either a contradiction or absurdity. Figures of speech and parables will be discussed further in *Appendix E: Basic Grammar*.

6. Identify Timeless Principles

You'll also want to look for clues to the timelessness of a given statement that might be expressing an enduring theological principle. God is the same God today that He was back when the Bible's authors penned their work. Sometimes Scripture defines God's responses to specific behavior going on in the past, but it may also reveal something about God's character that will never change. The psalmist wrote, "Before the mountains were born Or You gave birth to the earth and the world, Even from everlasting to everlasting, You are God" (Ps. 90:2) and the writer of Hebrews said Jesus is the same yesterday, today and forever (Heb. 13:8). God never changes, and He is everlasting. So is His Word!

For example, God continually reprimanded Israel for the nation's disobedience and worship of other gods. Eventually, God disciplined Israel by allowing other powerful nations like Assyria and Babylon to oppress and ultimately disperse the Jewish people. Do these examples apply to modern-day readers? Absolutely. God's message has always been to "have no other god's before me" (Ex. 20:3; Deut. 5:7). This command has never changed. We can do much to learn from the example of Israel's disobedience set out in Scripture.

Identify all possibilities of what the passage could mean, and then select the best option based on your observations. Choose what you think the author intended to convey. Then you can move on to compare other Bible translations.

7. Compare Multiple Translations

The Bible was originally written primarily in Greek and Hebrew. A small portion of the book of Daniel was written in Aramaic. The first person to translate the Bible into English from Latin was William Tyndale in the 16th Century. Today there are hundreds of different English versions of Bibles. Some stick as close as possible to the original meaning of the Greek, Hebrew or Aramaic word. However, some words do not have an exact English equivalent; these word-for-word translations often seem "wooden," and a bit unnatural.

Other translations attempt to communicate the exact thought and emotion of the original text. These translations will use the number of words necessary to reproduce the idea precisely in English. Some believe these thought-for-thought translations are more accurate as well as more understandable.

Consider the simple graphic below showing the difference in translations. The versions on the left are the most wooden, word-for-word translations. Moving right, the translations become more thought-for thought. (Note: The KJV follows the Septuagint, the Greek Old Testament, rather than the original Hebrew)

Proverbs 18:24	
KJV	A man that hath friends must shew himself friendly: and there is a friend that sticketh closer than a brother.
NASB	A man of too many friends comes to ruin, But there is a friend who sticks closer than a brother.
ESV	A man of many companions may come to ruin, but there is a friend who sticks closer than a brother.
NIV	One who has unreliable friends soon comes to ruin, but there is a friend who sticks closer than a brother.
NLT	There are "friends" who destroy each other, but a real friend sticks closer than a brother.
MSG	Friends come and friends go, but a true friend sticks by you like family.[41]

Word-for-word translations rely heavily on the actual words used by the authors as opposed to a paraphrased summation of the thought that could miss key details.   When comparing Bible translations, seek a good balance between word-for-word translations and thought-for-thought translations. Doing so will help you arrive at the most accurate interpretation.

The Importance of Word Studies

There is a final but very significant piece to proper interpretation: word studies. Because of the variety of Bible translations, it's important that you learn how to investigate word meaning for yourself. These can be the most rewarding experiences for serious Bible students.   One word can be packed with deep significance! Studying words in the original languages they are written in can shed tremendous light on the passage you are studying, and will protect you against misinterpretation. More on how to complete word studies will be addressed in *Chapter 7: Word Studies.*

The Bible is a Divine book that contains revelation of God's plan of redemption over all time. It is a book of mystery, intrigue, comfort, sorrow, encouragement and great joy. Above all, it communicates the heart of God. Interpreting it well is an awesome responsibility.

> *"A misinterpreted Bible is a misunderstood Bible."*
>
> *– Anonymous*

Once you arrived at what seems to be the most accurate interpretation you will be ready for the third and most personal step: application.

CHAPTER 4

APPLICATION:
HOW DO I RESPOND?

*"All Scripture is inspired by God and profitable for teaching, for reproof, for correction, for training in righteousness." – **2 Timothy 3:16***

I n Judaism, there is a beautiful prayer called the "Shema." It is the cry of the Jewish person's heart, the central prayer in the Jewish prayer book. The first line of the Shema reads:

Shema Israel, Adonai Eloheinu Adonai echad
Hear, O Israel, the Lord is our God, the Lord is One

Then, after a pause, Deuteronomy 6:5–9 is recited:

"You shall love the Lord your God with all your heart and with all your soul and with all your might. These words, which I am commanding you today, shall be on your heart. You shall teach them diligently to your sons and shall talk of them when you sit in your house and when you walk by the way and when you lie down and when you rise up. You shall bind them as a sign on your hand and they shall be as frontals on your forehead. You shall write them on the doorposts of your house and on your gates."

Notice the very first word in the *Shema* prayer: *Hear.* In Hebrew, this word for "hear," or "shema," is different than simply listening. *Shema* means, "listening with the intent to obey." It is active listening, or listening with the commitment to respond to whatever God says.

The relationship between hearing and obeying God's Word is what the third step of Inductive Bible Study—*application*—is all about. It is about choosing to believe the truth you've discovered, and allowing that truth to change your thinking and your conduct, and ultimately, your entire life.

It is impossible to know the Bible or the will of God without being willing and ready to obey it. Jesus taught this concept in John 17. Answering the Jews who were questioning how He could know so much Jesus said, "My teaching is not Mine, but His who sent Me. If anyone is *willing to do His will*, he *will know* of the teaching, whether it is of God or whether I speak from Myself" (John 17:17, emphasis added).

Are you willing? Will you follow through and do what the Lord asks? If you are, Jesus Himself promises you will come to know God better.

WHAT IS APPLICATION?

Application is the main reason for Bible Study: to *do* something with it. Anyone can read the Bible, and anyone can study it. But only those who are prepared to obey it will be transformed. Remember that the purpose of the Word of God is to change people into God's image, to be witnesses for Him to the world. Application is the step that stimulates this transformation.

Application gives permission for God's truth to move in and rearrange values, priorities, schedules, attitudes, actions, and even relationships. Simply put, it is applying what God is teaching you by asking, "How do I respond?"

A LESSON FROM JAMES

James, the half-brother of Jesus echoes this. He writes, "But prove yourselves doers of the word, and not merely hearers who delude themselves" (James 1:22).

This exhortation by James is rich with meaning. In this verse, the verb "prove" is a present imperative; it means it is a command to make something a habitual practice. James is teaching the importance of consistently doing or obeying the Word of God.

The word "hearers" in the original Greek language is *akroates*, which means "one who sits passively listening to a speaker." The Greek word for "delude" is *paralogizomai*. *Paralogizomai* means, "to continually mislead, deceive, or beguile oneself." James is warning those who choose to listen passively to the Word of God that they will be continually misled and deceived.

> *"Bible study is not complete until we ask ourselves, 'What does this mean for my life, and how can I practically apply it?'"*
> *– John MacArthur*

People spend their whole lives studying the Bible and may be full of facts and knowledge. However, if this is the end goal of studying the Bible, it's of no use for the believer. The true intent of Bible study, according to the apostle John is "that they may know You, the only true God, and Jesus Christ whom You have sent" (John 17:3).

Commit to being an active hearer of the Word of God, to listening with the intent to obey.

Helpful Questions to Ask

As you commit to "listening with the intent to obey," use the following questions to help you apply what you are learning:

> *"One step forward in obedience is worth years of study about it."– Oswald Chambers*

- How does this truth apply to my personal life—my family, my work, my church, and my community?

- Given this new understanding, what specific changes should I make in my life?

- What is my plan to carry out these changes, and when?

- What can I model and teach?

- What does God want me to explain or share with someone?

- What illustration or analogy can I develop to remember the truth it contains?

- How does this passage apply to me?

- Does this passage apply to a distinct group of people?

- Does this passage reflect a particular problem for that day and culture? If so, is it timeless?

- Is there a commandment of God I have ignored and need to consider?

- What should I ask God in regards to what I have learned?

- Does this passage of Scripture reveal any error in belief that I may have had about God?

- What personal changes should I make in light of this truth?

- How should I begin making these changes?

- How can I live what I have learned while facing a critical and sometimes harsh world?

"To obey is better than sacrifice..."
– 1 Sam. 15:22

- Is this truth charging me to reflect a part of God's character?

- What can I do to get more motivation and accountability to keep going?[6]

From these (and many more questions), you should be able to come up with some very clear, personal action statements. Action statements are what you are committing to do from what you have observed, interpreted and now want to apply. These statements should be personal, selective and specific.

Personal

These statements should contain the words "I will," to specify the action that will be taken. "I will forgive my friend for lying to me."

Selective

You simply won't be able to apply every principle you learn when you study your Bible inductively. Be selective when coming up with your action statements. Ask yourself: "Which of these principles touch on a very real need in my life?" Then, choose one or maybe two, and ask God how you should respond. Be careful to not ignore the others, or the ones you want to avoid. Sometimes those are the ones you should tackle first!

Specific

Your action statement should also be precise and specific. An action statement that says, "I will respond with respect to my boss who was demeaning," is much more specific than "I will be respectful."

L et's look at Romans 5:3–5 and consider one example of how to apply the passage personally:

"And not only this, but we also exult in our tribulations, knowing that tribulation brings about perseverance; and perseverance, proven character; and proven character, hope; and hope does not disappoint, because the love of God has been poured out within our hearts through the Holy Spirit who was given to us."

Asking the suggested questions from the list above (after observation and interpretation, of course!) could result in the following practical application for Romans 5:3–5:

> *"The goal of Inductive Bible study is not to make us smarter sinners, but to make us more like our Savior."*
> **– Dr. Howard Hendricks**

I will rejoice in this job loss because God is working something good out of it. I will memorize John 3:16 to remind myself how much God loves me so that I can cling to the truth that God has His best intentions in mind for me when I start to doubt. His love is bigger than my trial. I know that others are watching, and I want to be a witness to the hope I have in Christ! I will ask a trusted friend to walk through this with me to help me keep focused on the promises of God rather than my situation.

1. The action steps above are personal: *I will rejoice in this job loss.*

2. They are selective: *God's love is bigger than my trial.*

3. And, they are specific: *I will memorize John 3:16.*

Though it may seem tedious, the application process is what will begin to change your heart to be more in line with the heart of God. This is the purpose of Inductive Bible Study!

PITFALLS TO AVOID

I f your end-goal of Bible Study is "study for the sake of study," be careful. Focusing so much on the Scriptures at the expense of missing the One the Scriptures were written about is dangerous. At one point Jesus reprimanded the Jewish leaders for this very issue:

> *"You search the Scriptures because you think that in them you have eternal life; it is these that testify about Me and you are unwilling to come to Me so that you may have life."*
> *– John 5:39–40, emphasis added*

Those religious leaders had made a god out of the Scriptures. The anointed Messiah their Scriptures spoke of was right in front of them—the fulfillment of everything they were so diligently studying—and they couldn't see Him.

Never forget that the ultimate goal of Bible study, whether inductive or otherwise, is *to know God and His Son so that you might have life in Him.* Jesus emphasized this important truth in John 17 declaring, "This is eternal life, that they may know You, the only true God, and Jesus Christ whom You have sent." – John 17:3

Be careful to avoid substituting interpretation for application. Being able to describe what a text is about is not the same as personalizing it and asking how you should respond. You will also want to guard against substituting surface obedience for significant life-change.

Additionally, if God is leading you through His Word to repent of something, do not attempt to justify the sin. Deal with the issue with God, and experience freedom! Avoid rationalizing sin because it seems to be accepted in the times or culture you live; what may be acceptable and common within a particular culture may be very different from God's standard. And of course, always guard against using Scripture out of context and trying to make Scripture fit your theology.

RESPONSES TO APPLICATION

J erry Bridges writes, "As we search the Scriptures, we must allow them to search us, to sit in judgment upon our character and conduct."

Sometimes as you are observing, interpreting and applying a passage it will be clear God is moving you to deal with some unconfessed sin. The Word of God is "sharper than any two-edged sword" (Heb. 4:12). It penetrates the heart and reveals things you may not have even been aware of. The Word of God judges and reproves, and it exposes negative attitudes and actions. If this occurs, humbly bow before God and ask Him to forgive you for whatever it is He has revealed.

Other times, you may be moved to respond in faith, lived out through obedience. It is important to combine faith with what you read and hear. Genuine faith will obey, which demonstrates gratefulness and love for the Father. When this occurs, don't be afraid to step out and do what God is asking you to do! You will be blessed.

"But one who looks intently at the perfect law, the law of liberty, and abides by it, not having become a forgetful hearer but an effectual doer, this man will be blessed in what he does." – James 1:25, emphasis added

CHAPTER 5

MEMORIZING AND MEDITATING ON SCRIPTURE

"How sweet are Your words to my taste! Yes, sweeter than honey to my mouth!" – **Psalm 119:103**

P icture a bird's nest high up in a tree, filled with baby birds just hatched from their eggs. The mother bird has just returned from her quest for food. The screeching chicks wait expectantly for mom to drop in a worm or a bug, mouths gaping wide and turned up toward the sky. They are hungry.

King David, who wrote many of the Psalms, had a sincere love for the Word of God. In fact, he referred to the Scriptures as "sweet... to my taste, sweeter than honey to my mouth" (Ps. 119:103) and "more desirable than gold, yes, than much fine gold; Sweeter also than honey and the drippings of the honeycomb" (Ps. 19:10). Only the Word of God satisfied David's thirsty and hungry soul, which David said God "has filled with what is good" (Ps. 107:9). David longed for God's Word, as the baby birds longed for food from their mother.

> *"The word of God must be . . .nearer to us than our friends, dearer to us than our lives, sweeter to us than our liberty, and pleasanter to us than all earthly comforts."*
>
> *– John Mason*

Do you hunger and thirst for the Word of God? Do you long to taste the "sweetness of the Word" like David?

There are certain disciplines within the life of the believer that will enhance their study of the Scriptures and help them experience this "sweetness." Two of these disciplines include memorization and meditation. Though not one of the three steps to Inductive Bible Study, they are vital to the personal life of the disciple of Christ.

SCRIPTURE MEMORIZATION

J ust before Jesus' crucifixion, He left His disciples with encouragement for what was to come. At one point He said, "But the Helper, the Holy Spirit, whom the Father will send in My name, He will teach you all things, *and bring to your remembrance all that I said to you*" (John 14:26, emphasis added).

How can something be recollected unless it was previously stored in someone's memory? Analytical Bible Expositor John Butler writes, "The principle for believers is that the Holy Spirit helps us to remember Scripture and spiritual lessons. When a verse pops into the mind when teaching, preaching, studying or pondering a decision of some sort—it is not your memory that is bringing that text to your mind, but it is the prompting of the Holy Spirit that is doing it."

For the Holy Spirit to quicken someone's memory, however, they must have previously filed the Scripture in their minds. Butler continues, "The Holy Spirit is like the recall button on a calculator—if you do not put anything in the memory of the calculator, the recall button will not bring up any information."

At first, memorizing Scripture will feel like work, and it will take perseverance. However, once you taste the "sweetness" of the Word, a whole new world will open up. Many people who memorize Scripture speak of seeing things differently, and experiencing a joy previously unknown.

An acute awareness will replace boredom. Words or phrases in the Bible that were previously confusing will suddenly bring light and revelation to your mind and heart. Like David you will be able to cry, "The unfolding of Your words gives light; It gives understanding to the simple. I opened my mouth wide and panted, For I longed for Your commandments" (Psa. 119:130).

As Scripture memory becomes more routine messages from pastors and Bible teachers may seem clearer. Scripture memory will increase your knowledge, stimulate your desire to learn, and develop a hunger and thirst in you for deeper understanding.

Professor of Philosophy at the University of Southern California, Dallas Willard, wrote:

"Bible memorization is absolutely fundamental to spiritual formation. If I had to choose between all the disciplines of the spiritual life, I would choose Bible memorization because it is a fundamental way of filling our minds with what it needs. This book of the law shall not depart out of your mouth. That's where you need it! How does it get in your mouth? Memorization."

REASONS TO MEMORIZE

Christians should memorize Scripture because they are called and commanded to learn God's Word to learn more about Him, what He has done, what He will do in the future, and what the believer can do presently to lead a purposeful, abundant life. There are many, many reasons (and benefits) for memorizing Scripture. Below are some of the most important.

The Bible Commands It

The writers of the gospels, the epistles, and Jesus himself reference the fact that God's people should have the Word of God stored up in their hearts. Verses like, "*Have you never read* what David did when he was in need, and he and his companions became hungry?" (Mark 2:25, emphasis added) reveal Jesus expected His followers to know the Word! Paul wrote in Colossians 3:16 to "Let the word of Christ richly dwell within you," and God commanded the Israelites in Deuteronomy 11:18 to, "therefore impress these words of mine on your heart and on your soul." Yes, Christians are called by God Himself to know and memorize Scripture (see also: Josh 1:8; Ps. 1; 15; Isa. 8:12; 1 Peter 3: 13-22; 4:12).

Memorizing Scripture Will Renew Your Mind and Transform Your Life

Romans 12:2 says, "Do not be conformed to this world, but be transformed by the renewal of your mind, that by testing you may discern what is the will of God, what is good and acceptable and perfect." Keeping the truth of Scripture fresh in your mind will renew and restore your thoughts to be more in line with God's. Also, Paul said, "For WHO HAS KNOWN THE MIND OF THE LORD, THAT HE WILL INSTRUCT HIM? But we have the mind of Christ" (1 Cor. 2:16). These two verses alone reveal that to discern what the will of God is, you must know His Word; when you know His Word, your thoughts begin to be more of God's thoughts! Isn't that profound?

God poured His mind into the Word so that we would be able to receive it through the Word. In his book *Scripture by Heart,* author Joshua Choonmin Kang refers to the mind as more than a possessor of knowledge. He says it includes a variety of powers: consciousness, vigilance, concentration, perception and spiritual sensitivity. He writes, "An excellent mind can see through the 'window' of the soul."[38]

As you develop your perceiving skills through observation and interpretation, your mind will grow in sensitivity. You will begin to comprehend everything in a new light, with greater meaning, and in more depth.

Through Inductive Bible Study and habits such as memorizing Scripture, you will learn the mind of God. Human minds contain selfish plans and purposes (Prov. 20:5) but the Lord's thoughts and plans are perfect. Memorizing Scripture develops a godly perception of both intellect and soul, leading to the transformation and renewal of your mind.

Memorizing Scripture Develops Godly Wisdom

Godly wisdom is different from worldly wisdom. The core of wisdom lies in the ability to discern good and evil. It's the reaction that turns a crisis into an opportunity to respond wisely to all situations. Joshua knew the secret of true wisdom. "Now Joshua the son of Nun was filled with the spirit of wisdom, for Moses had laid his hands on him; and the sons of Israel listened to him and did as the Lord had commanded Moses" (Deut. 34:9). His wisdom came directly from the Lord: "For the LORD gives wisdom; From His mouth come knowledge and understanding" (Prov. 2:6). Godly wisdom comes only from the Word of God, found in the pages of the Bible.

Memorizing Scripture Matures the Believer

Many biblical authors apply the analogy of "milk" verses "solid food" to the Word of God. "Milk" likely refers to more fundamental truths or initial foundational teachings. Paul mentions this in his letter to the Corinthians saying, "I gave you milk to drink, not solid food; for you were not yet able to receive it" (1 Cor. 3:2). And 1 Peter 2:2 says, "like newborn babies, long for the pure milk of the word, so that by it you may grow in respect to salvation." There is a place for the new believer to be filled with the elementary teaching of the "pure milk of the word."

However, God calls His children to "grow in the grace and knowledge of our Lord and Savior Jesus Christ" (2 Pet. 3:18). In Hebrews 5 and 6, the writer chastises Christians for their spiritual immaturity. He uses words like "dull" and "sluggish" (5:11, 6:1) to communicate they should have already grown and advanced to a more mature understanding of the Scriptures. These deeper truths are the "solid food" Paul referenced in 1 Corinthians 3:2, as well as the writer of Hebrews who said, "For though by this time you ought to be teachers, you have need again for someone to teach you the elementary principles of the oracles of God, and you have come to need milk and not *solid food.*" This "solid food" includes the riches of the mysteries of Christ and the wonders of His prophetic Word.

Memorizing Scripture, alongside Inductive Bible Study, will help move you from the elementary teachings of the Bible to a more advanced and mature understanding of God's overall plan of redemption laid out in the pages of your Bible.

Memorizing Scripture Will Help You Triumph Over Sin, Temptation and Satan

Bible memorization is probably the single most effective weapon the believer has to combat sin and temptation.[22] Jesus Himself used God's Word to fend off Satan's temptations on the mountain, and so should every believer (Matt. 4:1-11). However, there may be times when you don't have your Bible on hand and you are confronted with Satan's lies and deception. Having a storehouse of truth in your mind and heart will provide you with a mighty sword of defense any time of the day, and in any circumstance, to guard you against slipping into sin. This is why the psalmist was able to write, "How can a young man keep his way pure? By keeping it according to Your Word" (Ps. 119:9) and "The law of his God is in his heart; his steps do not slip" (Ps. 37:31).

Memorizing Scripture Will Help You Communicate the Gospel to Unbelievers

Have you ever been with a friend having a casual conversation that suddenly turned spiritual with an open door for talking about Jesus? Have you found yourself feeling ill- equipped and unprepared to share the Gospel message? Store up Scripture in your mind, and even if you can't always recall the exact Words, the Holy Spirit will recall them for you in times of need. This is especially true when sharing the Gospel with unbelievers.

Start by memorizing just a few key verses that will lead a person to an understanding of their need for a Savior. Here are just a few:

> *"...God shows his love for us in that while we were still sinners, Christ died for us." – Romans 5:8, ESV*

> *"For the wages of sin is death, but the free gift of God is eternal life in Christ Jesus our Lord. – Romans 6:23*

"If you confess with your mouth Jesus as Lord, and believe in your heart that God raised Him from the dead, you will be saved" **– Romans 10:9**

Then, when God gives you opportunities to share what you believe to others, you will have a storehouse of truth to share.

Jesus Modeled Memorizing Scripture

Ultimately, Jesus memorized Scripture, so Christians should, too. Jesus mastered the Bible, knew the verses by heart, and interpreted the Old Testament in light of the history of redemption. Matthew 4:1-11 recounts Jesus' temptation experience with Satan in the wilderness. Jesus did not have a Bible on hand at that moment, and yet three times when He was tempted Jesus responded with the phrase, *"It is written…"*

> **Matthew 4:4** *– "It is written, 'Man shall not live on bread alone, but on every word that proceeds out of the mouth of God'"* **(quoting Deuteronomy 8:3).**

> **Matthew 4:7** *– "It is written, 'You shall not put the Lord your God to the test'"* **(quoting Deuteronomy 6:16).**

> **Matthew 4:10** *– "For it is written, 'You shall worship the Lord your God, and serve Him only'"* **(quoting Deuteronomy 6:13).**

Each time Satan tempted Jesus, Jesus refuted the temptation with truth from the Old Testament Scriptures. The result? Matthew 4:11 says, "Then the devil left Him; and behold, angels came and began to minister to Him." Jesus modeled not only the importance of knowing Scripture by heart but also the power of the Word to defend against the enemy.

PERCEIVED ROADBLOCKS

People concoct all kinds of reasons why they should not or need not memorize Scripture. Perhaps, you are one of those people. Common excuses include:

- I can't because my memory is poor

- I just do not have time

- I am too old

- I have tried this before, and I could not do it

- I am not a pastor or in leadership, so why do I need to?

Each of these excuses is just that: *an excuse.* Memorizing Scripture takes time and hard work, but disciples of Jesus should use their best efforts to memorize out of obedience, love and gratitude for who He is and what He has done. Trust the Holy Spirit to help you in your time of need.

> *"I am convinced that one of the greatest things we do is memorize Scripture."*
> *– Billy Graham*

Recall God's promise to you mentioned earlier in this chapter:

*"But the Helper, the Holy Spirit, whom the Father will send in My name, He will teach you all things, and bring to your remembrance all that I said to you." – **John 14:26***

Jesus promised the Holy Spirit will help you. What better encouragement do you need?

TECHNIQUES TO HELP

M any people think they simply cannot memorize Scripture. However, it is most likely an issue of interest or importance, rather than ability. Those same people likely have many songs from their teen years memorized word for word, various phone numbers and close friends' birthdays. People rehearse and memorize what they want to remember. Scripture memorization succeeds only to the degree a person wants it to succeed.[38]

The following are some simple techniques to help to in your commitment to memorize the Word of God:

1. Stick to one translation

2. Memorize the location, or what some call "the address" together with the verse (such as Mark 1:5) along with the passage so you won't forget where the passage can be found.

3. Learn the passage well. Don't memorize it for the moment, without being able to recite it from memory one week, one month or one year later.

4. Pick a different word or phrase from the verse to focus on. Repeat the verse five or ten times out loud, emphasizing that one word or phrase. Then move on to the next word and do the same. For example, let's look at Deuteronomy 6:13

   • First round: "**_You_** shall fear only the LORD your God; and you shall worship Him and swear by His name."

   • Second round: "You shall **_fear_** only the LORD your God; and you shall worship Him and swear by His name."

- Third round: "You shall fear **_only the LORD your God_**; and you shall worship Him and swear by His name."

Continue doing this through the end of the verse. This one simple method of memorizing will walk you through the passage using Inductive Bible Study methods more than you realize, as you focus on different words and contemplate the meaning of those words. This will naturally help with interpretation.

5. If you learn best by hearing, use a Bible App that recites the verses or chapter out loud or a CD that you can listen to in the car, at home or when you are exercising.

6. Visualize the words. Use word pictures to create a scene in your mind you can recall when remembering the verse.

7. Do not try and memorize and multi-task. It just doesn't work.

8. Write verses on index cards and strategically place them around the house: on your bathroom mirror, on your refrigerator, and in your purse or briefcase. That way you can refer to the verse or passage throughout the day, wherever you are.

9. Solicit a friend or family member who will commit to either keeping you accountable with what you are memorizing, or memorize the same passage with you.

WORDS OF CAUTION

B e guarded against memorizing verses or entire chapters incorrectly or out of context, which could lead to incorrect meaning and interpretation. Sometimes, too, when folks memorize large passages of Scripture they fall into a place of spiritual "pride." Be careful to memorize for the purpose of coming to know God your Creator more intimately, and not to be able to spout off Scripture to impress others.

"I know of no other single practice in the Christian life more rewarding, practically speaking, than memorizing Scripture... no other single exercise pays greater spiritual dividends! Your prayer life will be strengthened. Your witnessing will be sharper and much more effective. Your attitudes and outlook will begin to change. Your mind will become alert and observant. Your confidence and assurance will be enhanced. Your faith will be solidified."
— Chuck Swindoll, *Growing Strong in the Seasons of Life*

BIBLICAL MEDITATION

Once you begin to memorize passages of Scripture, something supernatural will happen without you even realizing it. As you work hard at storing up verses or whole chapters in your mind, and as the truths of these words begin to transform your thoughts, they will then "drop down" into your heart and become a piece of who you are. You will find your conduct, your attitude, your beliefs, your perception of the world and even your spoken words begin to change! This shift happens through another process closely related to memorizing: meditation.

Biblical meditation is different from worldly meditation taught by false religions. Chanting the mantra "Om," while sitting in a strange position is not biblical meditation, nor is focusing on emptying the mind of thoughts or images. Biblical meditation is never a state that you arrive at, nor is it a "detaching" of your mind.

"These words, which I am commanding you today, shall be in your heart."
— Deuteronomy 6:6

On the contrary, biblical meditation focuses on filling the mind and heart with more and more of one particular subject: the Word of God.

God promises to bless those who meditate on the Word of God. Before Joshua was to lead the Israelites into the Promised Land, God spoke to him saying:

"This book of the law shall not depart from your mouth, but you shall meditate on it day and night, so that you may be careful to do according to all that is written in it; for then you will make your way prosperous, and then you will have success.
— Joshua 1:8

The English word "meditate" in this verse is the Hebrew word *hagah* meaning, "to moan, mutter, meditate, speak, or murmur (in pleasure or anger). It also means to ponder, imagine, study, talk, or utter."

Meditating on God's Word, then, means thinking about a word, verse or a whole passage over and over. It is the act of filling one's mind and even one's mouth with it. Biblical meditation is about thinking, pondering, imagining, muttering, and speaking the Word of God.

John MacArthur writes that it is not enough just to study the Bible. "We must meditate upon it. In a very real sense we are giving our brain a bath; we are washing it in the purifying solution of God's Word" (John J. MacArthur, *The MacArthur Study Bible*, Thomas Nelson, 2013).

King David, whom God called "a man after [His] own heart," (Acts 13:22), proclaimed that he remembered and meditated on God while resting on his bed and throughout the night. He wrote in Psalm 63:6: "When I remember You on my bed, I meditate on You in the night watches." David also meditated on all of God's work in Psalm 143:5: "I remember the days of old; I meditate on all Your doings; I muse on the work of Your hands." And, David contemplated God's ways in Psalm 119:15: "I will meditate on Your precepts and regard Your ways."

David modeled biblical meditation by thinking about God's precepts, instruction and commandments over and over.

FOUR PROMISES FROM GOD

P salm 1:1-3 reveals four wonderful promises for the man or woman who practices biblical meditation. Let's look at these verses. The promises are italicized:

"How blessed is the man who does not walk in the counsel of the wicked,
Nor stand in the path of sinners,
Nor sit in the seat of scoffers!
But his delight is in the law of the Lord,
And in His law he meditates day and night.
He will be like a tree firmly planted by streams of water,
Which yields its fruit *in its seasoson*
And its leaf does not wither;
And in whatever he does, he prospers.*"

Every living thing is sustained by water; without it, it won't survive. In this passage, the first promise for the man who meditates on the Word is that he will be like a tree planted by "streams of the living water." Water is a metaphor for life in the Bible. Jesus referred to Himself as the "living water" (John 4:14; 7:38-38; Isa. 55:1).

Those who meditate on the Word will have this "water" in such abundance––the overflow of Christ in them––they will thrive in life.

The second promise for the person who meditates on the Word is that they will, "yield [its] fruit in season." The word "fruit" is the Hebrew word *pĕriy*, which can mean literal fruit or fruit as in offspring or children. However, in this passage it is likely speaking figuratively, of fruit of actions. Those who meditate on the Word of God will bring forth the fruit of the Spirit spoken of in Galatians 5:22-23: "…love, joy, peace, patience, kindness, goodness, faithfulness, gentleness, self-control."

The third promise is that the "leaf will not wither." To wither means to fade or to lose freshness, to dry or shrivel up. Your strength, vitality, and energy will not be squelched.

Finally, those who meditate on the Word will prosper. This does not mean simple meditation will result in wealth dripping out of your pocketbook! "Prosper" in Hebrew is the word *tsalach*. This word means to rush, advance, or prosper, to make progress, succeed, to be profitable, or to go over or through (as a river). Interestingly, the prophet Isaiah used this same Hebrew word to describe God's Word in Isaiah 55:11 (KJV):

"It [God's Word] shall prosper [tsalach] in the thing whereto I sent it."

Living water will pour in and out of those who meditate on the Word of God. They will bear spiritual fruit, they will remain strong, and the Word in them will "be profitable." F. B. Meyer writes, "Devout meditation on the Word is more important to soul-health even than prayer. It is more needful for you to hear God's words than that God should hear yours, though the one will always lead to the other."

"Let my meditation be pleasing to Him; As for me, I shall be glad in the Lord."
— Psalms 104:34

Ultimately, hearing God's voice is the objective of both memorizing Scripture and then meditating on it. Hunger for the Word, and allow it to fill your mind and transform your thoughts. As you meditate on what you are memorizing, your heart will be changed and be moved in alignment with those things that move God. As you mature in faith, you will move from milk to meat, and your faith will be strengthened.

CHAPTER 6

GETTING ORGANIZED

*"But all things must be done properly and in an orderly manner." – **1 Corinthians 14:40***

A.A. Milne, the creator of the revered animated character Winnie the Poo, understood the need for organization. In typical Winnie the Poo language he wrote, "Organizing is something you do before you do something, so that when you do it, it is not all mixed up." Oh, those are great words to live by! They are true for life, and they are true for Inductive Bible Study. The goal of Inductive Bible Study is to see biblical truths more clearly...not become "all mixed up!"

Tools of the Trade

Before you even start your first Inductive Bible Study, you'll need to spend some time getting organized. Begin by gathering a few things you will need to keep close at hand. Organize them in a way that works best for you.

Bibles

Above all, you'll need to have a Bible in your preferred version. It's a good idea to have two or three other versions to compare translations while you are interpreting passages. There are numerous online sources available where you can move from one version to another with a click of a button. Some excellent sites include www.inductivebiblestudyapp.com, www.biblegateway.org, www.biblehub.com, and www.blueletterbible.org.

If you are brand-new to studying the Bible and are intimidated at the thought of finding certain books of the Bible or verses, consider purchasing Bible indexing tabs for a nominal cost. You can find these in Bible bookstores or online.

Pens & Notebooks

If you choose to approach Inductive Bible Study without the aid of technology, then you'll also want to invest in a good set of pens and or pencils that do not bleed through the pages of your Bible and offer a variety colors for marking key words with symbols and art. Here are a handful of suggested sets:

- Pilot FriXion Ball Erasable Gel Pens, Fine Point, 8-Pack Pouch. These pens write smooth and erase and repeatedly rewrite without damaging the pages of your Bible.

- Sanford Sharpie Fine Point Pen Stylo, Assorted Colors, 12-Pack. These water and smear-resistant pens work great for key word marking and don't bleed through paper. These pens offer precise and consistent writing.

- Sakura 30064 6-Piece Pigma Micron Assorted Colors 005 Ink Pen Set. Micron pens write permanent, smooth, and skip-free and crisp with colors that leave consistent lettering and lines every time.

If you prefer working with pencils, the Crayola 24ct Erasable Colored Pencils are easy to erase and their color lasts.

Find a notebook that works for you, either a simple spiral notebook or a nicer journal. Your notebook will be the place where you will take notes on things the Lord is teaching you or things you want to remember. Many people use this notebook to create organizational charts for tracking their observations, interpretation, and application. Observation charts will be discussed later in this chapter.

Bible Commentaries

The serious Bible student should always perform Inductive Bible Study before ever consulting a commentary. Commentaries are written by human authors, so automatically there is the chance of biased comments embedded in the author's belief system and their approach to interpreting the Bible. However, after careful observation and interpretation, seeking insight from learned theologians through commentaries is a wise step.

It is important to note these commentaries should be from a conservative, literal perspective. This viewpoint becomes especially important when studying books of prophecy like Daniel, Ezekiel or Revelation. A good indicator for whether a commentary takes a conservative, literal approach is when the commentator does not replace Israel with the church.

> *"It is amazing how much light the Scriptures shed on the commentaries."*
> *– Anonymous*

Some sound commentaries include:

- *Bible Commentary* by David Guzik,

- *Verse-by-Verse Commentary* by Studylight,

- *Expository Notes on all 66 Books of the Bible* by Thomas Constable

- *Commentary on the Bible* by Adam Clarke

- *The Treasury of David* by C. H. Spurgeon

- *Jamieson, Fausset, and Brown's Commentary On the Whole Bible* by R. Jamieson

- *Ironside Commentaries* – any

- *Expositor's Bible Commentary* by D.A. Carson

- Commentaries by Doug Moo – any

- Commentaries by George Ladd – any

Bible Land Resources

"It will come about that every living creature which swarms in every place where the river goes, will live. And there will be very many fish, for these waters go there and the others become fresh; so everything will live where the river goes. And it will

come about that fishermen will stand beside it; from Engedi to Eneglaim there will be a place for the spreading of nets. Their fish will be according to their kinds, like the fish of the Great Sea, very many" **(Ezek. 47:9-10).**

This particular verse speaks of a future time when the Dead Sea (a body of water in Israel with a salt content of 33.7 percent[14] where nothing lives) will burst forth with life. Some are fortunate to have traveled to Israel and have seen the Dead Sea with their own eyes. But those who haven't can still make use of resources such as maps or pictures of biblical places, to bring these Scriptures to life and help with interpretation.

Including the Bible lands in Bible study will bring another level of understanding to the Bible and to accurate interpretation. Bible atlases afford much more than maps; they teach the importance of geography as it relates to history, archeology, topography, climate, and soils. Here are a few great atlases:

- *Zondervan Atlas of the Bible* by Carl G. Rasmussen. This atlas includes three-dimensional maps and photographic images to help the lands of the Bible come alive.

- *The Satellite Bible Atlas* by Bill Schlegel. This newer Bible atlas includes 85 full-page color maps. Biblical events are indicated on enhanced satellite imagery, accompanied by geographical and historical commentary.

- *The Sacred Bridge*: *Carta's Atlas of the Biblical World* by Anson F Rainey and R. Steven Notley. Though expensive, this excellent resource is detailed, scholarly and makes good use of original sources and languages.

- *Then and Now Bible Maps* by Rose Publishing

There are also many wonderful DVDs available. BiblePlaces.com sells an excellent five-volume DVD set called *Pictorial Library of Bible Lands* that offer thousands of stunning pictures of Jerusalem, Judah, the Dead Sea area, Galilee, and Samaria.

Finally, there are numerous books with photographs and illustrations of the Holy Land that may be of help. *The Story of the Holy Land: A Visual History* by Peter Walker or *The Holy Land: An Armchair Pilgrimage* by Mitch Pacwa are two excellent options.

Concordances & Dictionaries

Bible concordances are indispensable tools for Inductive Bible Study, handy for locating passages in the Bible to gain insight into what a word meant in the original Greek, Hebrew or Aramaic language. Concordances are not dictionaries, but the two go hand-in-hand.

Remember: Your goal in observation and interpretation is to discover the author's original intent. Though you may be able to dig up the precise meaning of a word from a good concordance, the definition you arrive at does not guarantee that is what the original author meant to convey by using it. The exact equivalence between different languages hardly ever exists, so be cautious when using your concordance.

Typically, concordances contain an alphabetical index of words in the Bible, followed by Bible references where the word occurs. Often Bibles will include a short concordance in the back matter of the book. However, there are more exhaustive concordances available such as Young's Analytical Concordance of the Bible, Vine's Expository Dictionary of New Testament Words and the classic Strong's Exhaustive Concordance of the Bible. There are also excellent online concordances, such as www.blueletterbible.com.

For the purpose of this book, we will focus on the *Strong's Exhaustive Concordance of the Bible* that uses the King James Version translation. Let's look at Judges 14:19 as an example. Judges 14:18 says, "And the Spirit of the LORD came upon him [Samson], and he went down to Ashkelon, and slew thirty men of them, and took their spoil, and gave change of garments unto them which expounded the riddle."

Say you want to understand what it meant that the Holy Spirit "came" upon Samson. The word "came" is listed as Strong's number h6743 צָלַח in Hebrew, and is transliterated *tsalach* (the same word in Chapter 5 meaning "to prosper"). Underneath each word entry, you will find a list of references where the word occurs. This word *tsalach* occurs 64 different times in the Bible, in the Hebrew concordance of the KJV.

You can then look up h6743 in your favorite Bible dictionary to learn more definitions, see other words translated from h6743, and obtain a quick glance at other verses that use this particular word. If you do this using an online dictionary, you can even hear how to pronounce the word the word in Hebrew. With a biblical dictionary, you will learn the word *tsalach* means, "pushed forward, rushed or advanced; broke out; to prosper."

The Spirit didn't "come" upon Samson in a gentle way. According to the correct meaning of the word, the Spirit pushed forward, rushed, advanced, or broke out upon Sampson. When arriving at the application step in Inductive Bible Study, you would then be able to ask yourself, "What does this text mean for me, and how should I respond?"

Could the Spirit be more active and powerful in your life than you thought? Would knowing this definition make you more confident knowing He's working powerfully with you too, advancing or pushing forward on your life? Using concordances and dictionaries to complete word studies will benefit you as you discover actual word meaning. Word studies will be discussed further in Chapter 7.

For links to resources that offer online Bible dictionaries, visit http://InductiveBibleStudyApp.com/bookextras.

Bible Encyclopedias

Bible encyclopedias include definitions and articles for thousands of words, phrases and terms used in the Bible. Dates, religious environments of the time, family life, customs, language, and literature are some of the information you will find. Each term is cross-referenced and linked to the verses where it is found to bring understanding to the word in context to its use in a specific verse in the Bible. These articles have been written to help those seeking a greater knowledge of biblical characters, events and places.[5]

Extra-Biblical Resources

Extra-biblical writings are non-biblical resources that have helped corroborate the people, places and events of the Bible, most notably the existence of Jesus. More than thirty extra-biblical sources mention Jesus within 150 years of His life![12] They are excellent supplemental resources for Inductive Bible Studies.

The *Talmud* is one example. The Talmud is a collection of Jewish teachings that were passed down from generation to generation amongst the Jews and then finally organized after the destruction of Jerusalem in AD 70. Below is an extract that mentions Jesus:

"On the eve of Passover, Yeshu [a Hebrew word referring to Jesus] was hanged. For forty days before the execution took place, a herald went forth and cried, "He is going forth to be stoned because he has practiced sorcery and enticed Israel to apostasy. Any one who can say anything in his favor, let him come forward and plead on his behalf." But since nothing was brought forward in his favor he was hanged on the eve of the Passover!"[35]

Not only does the Talmud reference Jesus, it mentions His crucifixion and the Jewish leadership's desire to stone Him! (See also John 8:58–59, 10:31–33, 39)

Another important extra-biblical source is Josephus, a Jewish historian who mentions more than a dozen biblical individuals and corroborates pivotal events in the life of Christ. For example, Josephus wrote:

"So these high priests did so upon the arrival of their feast which is called the Passover. On this day they slay their sacrifices from the ninth hour until the eleventh, with a company [phatria] of not less than ten belonging to every sacrifice -- for it is not lawful for them to have the feast singly by themselves -- and many of us are twenty in a company. These priests found the number of the sacrifices was two hundred and fifty-six thousand five hundred; which, if we

assume no more than ten feasted together, amounts to two million seven hundred thousand and two hundred persons..."

If you were going through the book of John and learning about the very last Passover Jesus celebrated on earth, the above quote from Josephus would give you great insight into the culture of that day around Passover. You would have an image of the sights, smells, and activities going on in Jerusalem that aren't communicated by the biblical writers.

Many other historical sources outside the Bible corroborate events within the Bible. Make use of the sources that best assist you in your studies!

Establish a Markup System

Key words are helpful ways to visualize certain aspects of the biblical text. Many Inductive Bible Study systems have distinct symbols they encourage you to use, but you don't have to adhere to one markup system. If you are creative and want to come up with your own, go for it! Whichever you choose, keep your list of symbols handy.

The Inductive Bible Study app allows users to create custom markings that can easily be applied to the text or users are free to use one

of its hundreds of suggested markings for key words. To view a comprehensive listing, visit http://InductiveBibleStudyApp.com/bookextras.

CREATE AND USE AN ORGANIZATIONAL CHART

A helpful tool when studying Inductively is an organizational chart. The organizational chart will be a place where you can write down and record all of your observations. Use it to document what you have learned or to list any lingering questions you have. An organizational chart will help you see visually all you are observing and interpreting, and be able to draw logical conclusions from those observations. You can also use this outline to make a written commitment to "do" what you have committed to God you are going to do with what you have learned.

By writing everything down in organized fashion, God's Word will become more clear and crisp. You will be able to record what God says to you, take more ownership in your learning, and experience greater transformation.

Basic Inductive Bible Study Chart

*"Watch the path of your feet And all your ways will be established." – **Proverbs 4:26***

Create your chart on a sheet of paper by dividing the paper into three sections. Label the first section Observation. Label the second section Interpretation, and the third Application. The first section should be the largest of the three, about half of the sheet. Split the other two sections so they take up the rest of the page equally.

Next, write down all of your observations from the passage or verse you are studying in the Observation section. Remember to study chapters and paragraphs first (context), and mark down what you have observed. Ask as many questions as possible about the passage, using the Big 6 Questions and additional lists of questions offered in Chapter 2. Don't answer those questions yet; rather, write down the context of the passage, noting what is written before and after the part you are studying. Note any other similar passages and add them to this section as well.

Now, answer the questions raised in the first section. Refer to a Bible encyclopedia to glean more insight into factual or historical data, and Bible atlases for the geographical background.

Take all of the information learned from the Observation section, and enter your interpretation of the passage in the second section. This is where you are applying meaning to the passage, what you have determined the author was trying to communicate.

Finally, in the third section, enter how you will apply what you have learned to your life. What main idea will you take away from the passage? What did you learn about God, other people or life in general from this passage? What will you do with what you have learned?

It may seem like meaningless work, but filling out this chart will not only keep your thoughts organized, but it will help solidify what you are learning in your mind and heart.

INDUCTIVE BIBLE STUDY CHART	
Bible Passage	
Observation	
Interpretation	
Application	

A free downloadable PDF version of the above chart can be found at http://InductiveBibleStudyApp.com/bookextras.

The writer of Proverbs wisely said, "The soul of the sluggard craves and gets nothing,

But the soul of the diligent is made fat" (Prov. 13:4). Be diligent for the Lord promises blessing for a little bit of perseverance and organization! Though you are putting in the hard work of charting your path before you begin, and then taking time to document what you observe, interpret and apply, be encouraged. Your work is being carried and directed by the Holy Spirit.

*"The mind of man plans his way, but the LORD directs his steps." – **Proverbs 16:9***

CHAPTER 7

WORD STUDIES

*"Take to your heart all the words with which I am warning
you today, which you shall command your sons to observe
carefully, even all the words of this law. For it is not an idle
word for you; indeed it is your life. And by this word you will
prolong your days in the land, which you are about to cross the
Jordan to possess." –* **Deuteronomy 32:46-47**

Words are the foundation for meaning, the building blocks to all communication. Theologian J. Vernon McGee observed: "From an alphabet you make words, and Jesus Christ is called the 'Word of God'–the full revelation and intelligent communication of God. He is the only alphabet we can use to reach God."

Any given word may have a range of meaning. Biblical word studies seek to discover the original meaning of words as the author intended. Remember that words function in a context, especially when interpreting Scripture. The aim of word study in exegesis (interpretation) is to try to understand as precisely as possible what the author was striving to convey by his use of a word in a particular context.

Words do not exist in a vacuum. Their meaning is affected by history and culture, sometimes changing from one generation to the next. This principle even impacts biblical lexicons (dictionaries). Those who assemble dictionaries do so based on two things: their hypotheses regarding how a word was used in different contexts, and their opinions. In other words, simply looking up the meaning of a Hebrew or Greek word in dictionary won't be enough to assure accurate translation. It will take a bit of work!

Because of this, your own biblical word studies must always be performed with great regard and awe for the words' actual Author— Jesus Christ—and a leaning on His Spirit. Only this will protect you from coming up with meaning different than what the Spirit intended in a given passage.

Because the Bible is written primarily in Hebrew and Greek, it will be beneficial for you to learn how to perform Hebrew and Greek word studies during Inductive Bible Study. These will become additional tools to help you glean the full meaning of what you are studying. Let's start by learning how to complete a Hebrew word study.

The Old Testament, what the Jews refer to as the *Tanakh*, was written primarily in Hebrew with a small portion of Daniel written in Aramaic. Performing any word study involves dissecting words in their original language—in this first case, Hebrew.

To perform a word study for a Biblical Hebrew word you will need a few things: a Hebrew text, a Hebrew-English lexicon, and a concordance.

The Hebrew Text

The *Biblia Hebraica Stuttgartensia* (BHS) is most theologians' first choice for studying the Hebrew Masoretic text. You can also refer to an English translation that includes words keyed to Strong's numbers (such as the *AMG Hebrew Key Word Study Bible*). An excellent option is John Kohlenberger's *Interlinear NIV Hebrew-English Old Testament*. Online research tools such as BibleWorks or Blue Letter Bible also often provide a Hebrew-English interlinear mode.

A Concordance

Concordances provide the rate of recurrence and the range of usage for words. The *Englishman's Hebrew Lexicon and Concordance* by George V. Wigram is coded to Strong's and helpful for confirming (or nullifying) the definitions of a lexicon. This resource also helps determine the recurrence of various meanings.

A Hebrew Lexicon

A lexicon contains the definition and etymology of a selected word. It is basically a biblical dictionary. Some options include *The New International Dictionary of Old Testament Theology and Exegesis* (5 volume set) by Willem A. VanGemeren, the *Theological Wordbook of the Old Testament* by Harris, Archer and Waltke, and *A Concise Hebrew and Aramaic Lexicon of the Old Testament* by William Lee Holladay.

There are three simple steps for conducting a Hebrew word study. We will use word "hem" from the NIV version of Psalm 139:5, "You _hem_ me in behind and before, and you lay your hand upon me."

1. First, look up the word "hem" in your concordance.

2. Note the corresponding Strong's number for the word "hem" for that verse (if there are more Strong's numbers, write them down as well). In this case, it is Strong's number h6696, and the Hebrew word צוּר *tsuwr.*

3. Next, lookup the corresponding number(s) in your lexicon. You will learn that *tsuwr* means: to confine (in many applications, literally and figuratively, formative or hostile); to fortify, enclose, lay siege, shut in, or put up in bags. Exodus 23:22, Deuteronomy 2:19, 20:2, 19, and Judges 9:31 are verses that also use this same word in relation to besieging a city.

4. After consulting commentaries to affirm your findings, you can correctly interpret this verse to mean God constructs a fortification around His children, or literally besieges his children. God confines His people in a place of safety. Make sure to base your decision on the context of the verse. For Psalm 139:5, this definition seems to be appropriate.

CONCORDANCE SAMPLE		
H6696 (רוּצ *tsuwr*) – translated "hem" in the NIV translation		
Verse	**English Word Used**	**Scripture excerpt (KJV)**
Dt 20:12	Besiege	war against thee, then thou shalt **b** it:
2Sa 20:15	Besieged	And they came and **b** him in Abel of
Dt 2:9	Distress	And the LORD said to me, **D** not the
Neh 2:17	Distress	Then said I unto them, Ye see the **d**
Dt 14:25	Bind	it into money, and **b** up the money in
Ezk 5:3	Bind	in number, and **b** them in thy skirts,
Jdg 9:31	Fortify	Behold they **f** the city against the.
1Ki 7:15	Cast	For he **c** the two pillars of brass, of
Song 8:9	Inclose	We will **i** her with boards of cedar.
Ps 139:5	Beset	Thou hast **b** me behind and before,

HEBREW LEXICON SAMPLE	
Translated "hem" in the NIV translation	
Strong's Number	6696
Original Word	רוּצ
Word Origin	a primitive root
Transliterated Word	Tsuwr
Phonetic Spelling	Tsoor
Parts of Speech	Verb

Definition	1. to bind, besiege, confine, cramp
	    a. to confine, secure
	    b. to shut in, beseige
	    c. to shut up, enclose
	 2. to show hostility to, be an adversary, treat as foe
	 3. to form, fashion, delineate

*"Word studies must be done not in isolation but in conjunction with the passage, context and their relation to the other words that structure the sentence or section, lest a wrong meaning is given to a word because the same word can be used in different ways." – **Pastor Xavior Ries, Calvary Chapel Pasadena***

Hellenistic (Greek) culture was pervasive in Israel before, during and after Jesus' time here on earth and all of the ancient textual evidence corroborates that the New Testament was written in Greek. Many foundational doctrines in the New Testament revolve around a single English word, such as faith, grace, redemption, justification, gospel, or sanctification. To fully understand these great doctrines of the faith, it should behoove the student to study specific Greek words connected to that doctrine to derive their fullness of meaning.

When performing Greek word studies, like Hebrew, it is imperative to pay close attention to the context in which the word is used. This stipulation should not be surprising, for even in English, context is critical to understand what a given word means. For example, take the word "trunk." The phrase "Look at the trunk" could refer to some different things: the trunk of an elephant, the trunk of a car, the trunk of a tree or a storage trunk. To understand the true meaning of "trunk," you'd need to examine the context. This principle also applies to Greek word studies.

Greek words have more than one meaning, and meaning is determined by context. Words can mean only one thing at a time, so the student's job is to discover the original writer's single intended meaning. Be cautious about using the definition you uncover to force the verse mean what you want it to mean. If the definition you prefer makes the verse difficult to understand, you have likely adopted a definition that is not compatible with the context of the verse you are studying.

To perform Greek word studies, you will need some resources on hand: a concordance and a lexicon.

A Greek Lexicon

Again, lexicons are dictionaries. Three great resources for Greek word studies are *The English Lexicon of the New Testament* by Bauer, Arndt, and Gingrich, *The New Thayer's Greek-English Lexicon*, and *The New Analytical Greek Lexicon*.

A Greek Concordance

Strong's Exhaustive Concordance (KJV), the *NRSV Exhaustive Concordance* (1991), *Nelson's Complete Concordance (RSV),* the *New American Standard Exhaustive Concordance of the Bible,* or the *Englishman's Concordance* are a few options available at online bookstores.

The *New Englishman's Greek-English Concordance with Lexicon* is another option that combines a concordance with a lexicon.

Doing a Greek word study is not as difficult as it might seem. We will use the word "servant" as an example.

1. Choose a word from the text you are studying and look it up in a Strong's exhaustive concordance that matches your Bible's translation. For example, in Titus 1:1 Paul identifies himself as a "servant of God." Looking up the word "servant" in Strong's, you will find with Titus 1:1 the number associated with it is 1529.

2. Now look up this number in a Greek lexicon (some concordances have lexicons in the back of the book).

3. You will see Strong's number 1529, δοῦλος (Gr), occurs 124 times. 54 times it is translated as "servant," 18 times as "slave," 11 times as "slaves," two times as "servants," and one time as "slavery."

4. Figure out the range of meaning is for the word. You can do this by consulting word study books. The Theological Dictionary of the New Testament, Abridged in One Volume translated into English by F.F. Bruce is a sound resource. Another excellent resource is The NIV Theological Dictionary of New Testament Words. Consulting commentaries, journal articles, and authoritative websites will help you affirm the semantic range.

5. Make your decision based on context.

Online Resources

The steps in doing a word study, whether Hebrew or Greek, are basically the same whether you are using books or your computer. Online resources, however, have made the job so much easier. www.crosswalk.com, www.netbible.com, and www.blueletterbible.org are a few of the many resources available to you

Let's look at an example using the Inductive Bible Study App referencing Romans 11:25 (KJV):

*"For I would not, brethren, that ye should be ignorant of this mystery, lest ye should be wise in your own conceits; that blindness in part is happened to Israel, until the **fullness** of the Gentiles be come in."*

In this verse where Paul is speaking to Gentile believers, what does this word "fullness" mean?

By simply tapping the verse, a popup will appear providing you the option to view the verse details. The verse details screen lists the entire verse in the KJV, with appropriate Strong's numbers next to those words. This saves incredible time and resources! You can see the word "fullness" at the bottom of the screen is Strong's G4138. It is the Greek word, πλήρωμα, and the transliterated (pronounceable word) is *plērōma*.

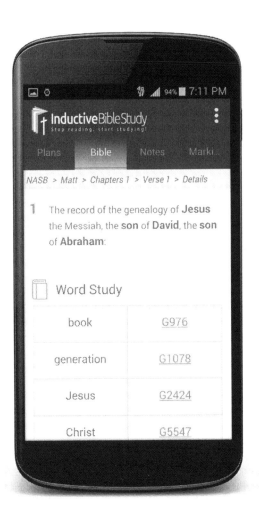

Clicking on the Strong's number will open up another screen that breaks this down even further. Notice now the Greek transliteration, *plērōma* is displayed with its pronunciation guide, and you can see the word is a neutral noun. You can read its definition: "that which is (has been) filled." The definition also includes an outline of the word's biblical usage to help unearth many possible definitions of this word: "a ship inasmuch as it is filled (i.e. manned) with sailors, rowers, and soldiers," or "in the NT, the body of believers, as that which is filled with the presence, power, agency, riches of God and of Christ."

After doing a complete study (incorporating dictionaries, commentaries, etc.) on the word "fullness," it seems clear Paul may not be talking about a specific number of Gentiles that need to accept Jesus before the veil is removed from the Jews' hearts, but a fullness of time. Some commentators believe it may be a fullness of understanding.

Another important resource at your fingertips is cross-referencing.

P art of understanding a verse's context is to find other verses that talk about the same thing. This is called cross-referencing, and this simple exercise will increase your understanding of a passage and even a word. In your Bible, you may see a small superscript letter next to a word. That is a cross-referencing system that will take you to other verses with similar words or ideas. Cross-referencing connects you to other verses that discuss the same point. Some Bibles have a center column listing these cross-referenced verses, and some list these verses down the side.

The Inductive Bible Study App allows students of the Bible to easily perform cross-referencing on any word found in the text.

The *Thompson Chain-Referencing system* and *Nave's Topical Bible* referencing system allow individuals to see cross-references as well. Nave's doesn't link verse to verse, but takes ideas—say on "hope"—and then lists verses that talk about the concept of hope. This resource doesn't necessarily connect you with verses with the same words, but with the same concepts.

A word of caution: Sometimes the verse listed is not always a cross-reference to a whole verse but only part of a verse. You may be studying John 3:16 for example and Nave's will send you to cross references that connect to the end of 3:16. If you are looking at the beginning of 3:16, you need to be careful knowing this cross-referencing may be to certain sections.

APPENDIX A
TYPOLOGY

"In the Old Testament the New Testament lies hidden; in the New Testament the Old Testament stands revealed."
– Augustine

There are many things that may seem odd or unclear in the Old Testament. Why did God require the Israelites to perform so many blood sacrifices? Why was there so much detailed instruction from God on how to build the Tabernacle, and later, Solomon's temple? Most of the time it is because God established those objects, events, or even people for a very important purpose. They were a shadow, pointing toward the reality in Christ.

"Therefore no one is to act as your judge in regard to food or drink or in respect to a festival or a new moon or a Sabbath day— things which are a mere shadow of what is to come; but the substance belongs to Christ." – **Colossians 2:16-17**

This is the idea of types, or "typology." Bob Smith, the author of *Basics of Bible Interpretation*, writes that a type is a premeditated resemblance that God has built into the Bible and history to illustrate and teach truth—to make it easier to grasp than if it were only stated in prosaic (prose) and propositional terms. It is a kindness of God to stir our minds and imagination by the use of types—to make an unforgettable impress. Smith sees it as God's way of "putting His brand on our brain" so that we cannot escape the impact of truth.

Though the word "typology" is not in the Bible, the word "type" is. It is derived from a Greek term *tupos*, which means a mark from a blow, or a print, figure, pattern, fashion, manner, form, or an example. Simply put, a type is an object, person, event or activity in the Old Testament God uses to point to Christ or some aspect of redemption and its fulfillment (antitype) in the New Testament.

Type/Antitype

Jesus used the concept of typology to point out who He was in the Scriptures, but never once used the word "type." Recall Jesus' response to Nicodemus in John 3:14. Nicodemus, a Pharisee who secretly approached Jesus at night, asked Jesus how it is possible to be born again. Jesus' answer included a reference to this Old Testament type: "As Moses lifted up the serpent in the wilderness, so must the Son of Man be lifted up" (John 3:14; Numbers 21:9).

This allusion to His crucifixion, the serpent on the pole, is the type—a draft or sketch of some important feature of redemption. To be a true "type," it must in some clear way resemble its antitype—in this case, the crucifixion itself. The anti-type is the answer or counterpart of the type.

In the New King James Version of 1 Peter 3:18-21, the word "antitype" is used to show the resemblance between Noah, the flood and the ark, and baptism: "For Christ also suffered once for sins, the just for the unjust, that He might bring us to God, being put to death in the flesh but made alive by the Spirit, by whom also He went and preached to the spirits in prison, who formerly were disobedient, when once the Divine longsuffering waited in the days of Noah, while the ark was being prepared, in which a few, that is, eight souls, were saved through water. There is also an antitype that now saves us—baptism (not the removal of the filth of the flesh, but the answer of a good conscience toward God), through the resurrection of Jesus Christ."

Thus, the antitype perfectly embodies the shadow of the type.

OTHER WORDS TO DESCRIBE TYPES

Scripture uses several other words to suggest the idea of correspondence or resemblance in addition to types, such as copy, shadow, illustration, form, or example. Here are a few verses that reflect this:

- "Nevertheless death reigned from Adam until Moses, even over those who had not sinned in the likeness of the offense of *Adam, who is a type of Him who was to come*." *– Romans 5:14*

- "For the Law, since it has only a shadow of the good things to come and not the very *form* of things, can never, by the same sacrifices which they offer continually year by year, make perfect those who draw near." *– Hebrews 10:1*

- "Who serve unto the *example and shadow* of heavenly things, as Moses was admonished of God when he was about to make the tabernacle" *– Hebrews 8:5, KJV*

- "Therefore no one is to act as your judge in regard to food or drink or in respect to a festival or a new moon or a Sabbath day—things *which are a mere shadow* of what is to come; but the substance belongs to Christ." *– Colossians 2:16-17*

- "The Holy Spirit was showing by this that the way into the Most Holy Place had not yet been disclosed as long as the first tabernacle was still functioning. *This is an illustration* for the present time, indicating that the gifts and sacrifices being offered were not able to clear the conscience of the worshiper." *– Hebrews 9:8-9, NIV*

THREE PREREQUISITES TO TYPOLOGY

F or typology to be true, there are three things that must be present.

A Natural Connection. The things being compared must consent with one another, or resemble or connect naturally. For example, the Passover Lamb in Exodus 12:3-13 is the type. Its blood provided salvation from the Egyptian plague, which corresponds with the antitype in 1 Corinthians 5:7, Jesus Christ, the true Passover Lamb: "For Christ our Passover also has been sacrificed."

Historically True. To be a true type, the people, object, event or activity must not be a symbolic representation. These things must have occurred historically in the Old Testament. Overlooking the historicity leads to problems, specifically of allegorizing or spiritualizing the type or antitype.

Predictive. Types always prefigure something future. Just as a prophet uttered predictive prophecy, so too is the type predictive of something yet to come.

Based on the Literal Meaning of a Text. Most importantly, a type must come from interpreting the passage literally. Springing from that literal meaning, however, is a foreshadowing of someone or something yet to come.[28]

A SAMPLING OF TYPOLOGY IN THE OLD TESTAMENT

T he Old Testament is pregnant with people, historical events, and objects that foreshadow things to come.

People – These are biblical characters whose lives and experiences illustrate some principle or truth of redemption. Examples of these types include:

- Adam. Scripture describes Adam as the "figure of him that was to come" in Romans 5:14, KJV.

- Melchizedek. Many theologians believe Melchizedek is a pre-incarnate appearance of Christ. This is expressed in Hebrews 6:20: "[Jesus] has become a high priest forever, in the order of Melchizedek" (NIV).

- Moses, whose mission was to redeem Israel out of slavery to Egypt expressed in Jesus and the redemption of man through his blood, the forgiveness of sins (Eph. 1:7).

- Joseph. Beloved of his father Jacob, Joseph was unjustly accused, rejected by his brethren and ultimately not recognized by his family (Gen. 37:1-50:26). So too was Jesus.

Historical Events – These are great historical events that became foreshadowing in the Bible of good things to come. Some examples of historical events include:

- Cities of Refuge. In the Bible, God established places called, "cities of refuge" where someone who accidentally killed another, who deserved death, could flee to find refuge and protection from death (Josh. 20:2-4). Jesus also provides refuge from spiritual death for those who believe in Him.

- The Wilderness Journey. Israel's disobedience led to God's holding them in the desert for forty years (Judg. 11:16), known as the wilderness journey. The antitype is revealed in the New Testament in the book of Hebrews: "Today, if you hear his voice, do not harden your hearts as you did in the rebellion" (Heb. 3:15 NIV). Believers today may end up "wandering" in the desert for lack of obedience.

Ritual Objects – These are persons, places, times, things, and actions in the Old Testament that also point toward the fulfillment in Christ.

- *Offerings.* Each offering—the burnt, sin, peace, grain and trespass offering each point to some aspect of Jesus' ministry on earth.

- *Trumpets* – Throughout the Old Testament, trumpets were used to sound an alarm, call people to an assembly, or announce a new moon. In the New Testament reality, the sound of the trumpet is associated with the voice of God (Matt.24:31).

- *The Tabernacle.* God gave Moses specific directions for how to construct the tabernacle in the desert. Later the writer of Hebrews makes it clear this was a pattern for the real Tabernacle in heaven: "They serve at a sanctuary that is a copy and shadow of what is in heaven" (Heb. 8:5 NIV).

Finally, one of the most profound studies in typology can be found in a study of the biblical feasts found in Leviticus 23. The Feast of Tabernacles, the last of the seven feasts, was the final feast on the Jewish calendar. God commanded the Israelites to erect temporary dwelling places and live in them for seven days. They were to remember the time when the presence of God dwelt among God's people in the wilderness in the tabernacle. The antitype pictures a day in the future when Jesus will once again dwell on earth with His people, ruling and reigning from Jerusalem.

APPENDIX B
INTERPRETING PROPHECY

Interpreting prophecy needs to be done with special care, deep reverence and a sincere dependence on the Holy Spirit. All prophecy will come to pass, whether it has already been fulfilled in the past, is being fulfilled in this day, or will be fulfilled in the future.

The book of Numbers affirms this. God's character is one of truth; He cannot be anything but truthful. Everything God says will happen in the Bible will occur. The book of Numbers says:

"God is not a man, that He should lie, Nor a son of man, that He should repent; Has He said, and will He not do it? Or has He spoken, and will He not make it good?" – **Numbers 23:19**

Because about half of the prophecies in the Bible have already been fulfilled in some literal way, and because God does not lie (it goes against His character), it follows that interpreting prophecy that has yet-to-be-fulfilled should also be interpreted from a literal standpoint.[50]

William Tyndale, an English scholar who translated the New Testament into English, said this: "Scripture has but one sense, which is the literal sense." This is true for Scripture in general, but especially prophetic passages. To interpret prophecy outside of it's literal meaning will lead the student to misinterpretation; it will distort God's promises.

Anthony Garland in his document *A Testimony of Jesus Christ* writes: "God's promises involve both ends of the communication channel: the things God said and what those who received His promises understood them to mean in the original context. It is not permissible, after the fact, to make what God said mean something different which would have been entirely foreign to those who originally received His word."

This is what happens when the interpreter tries to allegorize and spiritualize prophecy.

FOUR TIMES PERIODS OF BIBLICAL PROPHECY

When an Old Testament prophet spoke a prophetic word, he was referring to (though not knowingly) four time periods. It may have been the time the prophet was currently living in, the time Israel was in captivity in Babylon or just after their restoration to Israel after being released, the time of Jesus' first advent, or the time of his second advent (yet future).

Dual Fulfillment Prophecies

A prophecy may also have "dual fulfillment." A good example of dual fulfillment is the prophecy of the destruction of Babylon in Jeremiah 50:51. Though this indeed happened historically, its core complete fulfillment will occur in the last days (Rev. 18).

Time Gaps

A prophecy may also have a significant time gap between when certain aspects of prophecies are fulfilled. For example, in Luke

4:17 Jesus read from the Isaiah scroll in His hometown of Nazareth, telling his hearers "Today this Scripture has been fulfilled in your hearing" (Luke 4:21). He read:

> *"The Spirit of the Lord is upon Me,*
> *Because He anointed Me to preach the gospel to the poor.*
> *He has sent Me to proclaim release to the captives,*
> *And recovery of sight to the blind,*
> *To set free those who are oppressed,*
> *To proclaim the favorable year of the Lord."*
> **– Luke 4:18-19**

This was verbatim from Isaiah 61:1-2a. However, Jesus stopped just short in Luke 4 of Isaiah 61:2b which reads, *"And the day of vengeance of our God."* Why is this?

This portion of Isaiah speaks of Jesus' first and second advents. Jesus has preached the gospel to the poor, given freedom to captives and given sight to the blind. However, the "day of vengeance of our God" is a prophecy that has yet to be fulfilled, and won't be until He returns to rule and reign from the New Jerusalem on earth. This time gap in fulfillment does not mean the prophecy will not be completely fulfilled. It just hasn't happened yet.

Complete and Final Fulfillment

Finally, a prophecy may have its complete and final fulfillment only in the future, with the restoration of God's Kingdom on earth, and the rule and reign of King Jesus.

INTERPRETING APOCALYPTIC LITERATURE

A pocalyptic literature was a form of literature prevalent during the seventh and sixth centuries BC, in both the pagan nations surrounding Israel and among Israel itself.

This happens to be when the Old Testament apocalyptic literature was revealed and documented.

Apocalyptic literature is a form of biblical prophecy that frequently contains eccentric descriptions and bizarre imagery that predict disaster and destruction. The writers often received odd dreams and visions that they then communicated to Israel. They also proclaimed words of encouragement with an emphasis on salvation, the end of days, the deliverance of the righteous, and coming punishment for the wicked. The books of Daniel, Ezekiel and Zechariah in the Old Testament contain elements of this type of literature. In the New Testament, 2 Thessalonians 2, Mark 13, and Matthew 24 also contain apocalyptic elements. John's entire Revelation is apocalyptic. In fact, The Greek word *apokalypsis*, from which "apocalyptic" means, "an unveiling" or "disclosure." For biblical apocalyptic literature, God is thus unveiling or revealing something. The interpreter should keep this in mind.

Apocalyptic literature makes use of heavy symbolism, sometimes describing "other-worldly" activities, objects or events that typically convey a deeper message. The terrible, iron-toothed beast of Daniel 7, the long-haired locusts with men's faces of Revelation 9, and the four-faced creatures of Ezekiel 1 are just a few of the bizarre images that Bible interpreters attempt to make sense of!

It is important when interpreting apocalyptic literature to differentiate between the medium (the channel or vehicle) and the message. Acknowledge the vehicle (the prophet, angel, etc.) God chose to communicate the message, but then focus your attention on the hermeneutics (interpretation). Guard against becoming so infatuated with the amazing symbolism and all of the things those symbols or metaphors could mean, that you become detracted from the message.

*"And he that sat was to look upon like a jasper and a sardine stone: and there was a rainbow round about the throne, in sight like unto an emerald." – **Revelation 4:3, KJV***

APPENDIX C
BIBLICAL GENRES

Narrative Literature. Narratives—or stories—comprise more than forty percent of the Old Testament. Narrative literature needs to be interpreted in its historical context; otherwise, there is too much possibility of misinterpretation. The following Old Testament books include large amounts of narrative matter: Genesis, Joshua, Judges, Ruth, 1 and 2 Samuel, 1 and 2 Kings, 1 and 2 Chronicles, Ezra, Nehemiah, Daniel, Jonah, and Haggai. However, Exodus, Numbers, Jeremiah, Ezekiel, Isaiah, and Job contain significant narrative sections as well.

Law. The Law (or the Torah in Hebrew) is the first five books of the Hebrew Scriptures (in Greek, the Pentateuch): Genesis, Exodus, Leviticus, Deuteronomy, and Numbers. These books are mostly narratives (see below) of the story of the beginning of the world to Moses' death, sprinkled with God's code of law. When interpreting the Law/Torah, look for the principle behind the statement in the law and try to apply that—especially if the command is not reiterated in the New Testament.

Wisdom Literature. Typical wisdom literature in the Old Testament is most often not absolute truths or promises. For example, Solomon's proverb, "Train a child in the way that he should go, and when he is old he will not turn from it" (Prov. 22:6 KJV) is not a promise from God this will always happen, but a general truth based on examination. Job, Psalms, Proverbs and Ecclesiastes and Song of Solomon are considered wisdom literature.

Poetry. These books relate to Israel's spiritual life and cross over with wisdom literature. These books also include Job, Psalms, Proverbs, Ecclesiastes and Song of Solomon. Hebrew poetry relies on parallelism, unlike English poetry that emphasizes rhyme and meter, and figures of speech.

Historical. These twelve books relate to Israel's national life and development. They include: Joshua, Judges, Ruth, 1 & 2 Samuel, 1 & 2 Kings, 1 & 2 Chronicles, Ezra, Nehemiah, and Esther. Much of ancient Israel's formation, rise to prominence, collapse into moral and physical defeat, and restoration is included in these books. Many of the most famous characters in the Bible—people like David, Elijah, Solomon, Ahab, Esther, and many others—make their appearance in this section.[27]

Apocalyptic. These books include Daniel, Ezekiel and Zechariah. Typical apocalyptic literature involves prophets who communicate God's truth and prophecy often through bizarre imagery. Wild and unusual dreams and visions are common, and the imagery is often focused on eschatological (end times) events and people.

INTERPRETING LITERATURE OF THE NEW TESTAMENT

Historical Books. Historical books in the New Testament include Matthew, Mark, Luke, and John (the gospels), and Acts. The most important thing to ask when interpreting the gospels is "who is the audience?" Matthew was written to a primarily Jewish audience, and this gospel must be understood with that in mind. Mark wrote to the Greeks, and John to the Gentiles. Interpret the gospels individually, but also consider why one gospel flows to the other. The gospels are the transition between the Old and New Covenants. A good portion of the gospels and much of Acts is narrative.

Parables. Parables are figures of speech--stories used to depict a spiritual truth often hard for people to understand. Jesus often taught using parables, and this was foretold in the Old Testament: "Listen, O my people, to my instruction; Incline your ears to the words of my mouth. I will open my mouth in a parable; I will utter dark sayings of old" (Ps. 78:1-2).

Epistles. Epistles are letters primarily written by Paul to the fledging Gentile churches and people within those churches. The Pauline epistles—those written by the apostle Paul—include: Romans, 1 Corinthians, 2 Corinthians, Galatians, Ephesians, Philippians, Colossians, 1 Thessalonians, 2 Thessalonians, 1 Timothy, 2 Timothy, Titus, and Philemon. The non-Pauline epistles include: Hebrews, James, 1 Peter, 2 Peter, 1 John, 2 John, 3 John, Jude, and Revelation.

Many of these letters contain exhortation (and sometimes discipline) that is applicable for believers today. Paul makes use of logical connectors and conjunctions bridging the relationships of clauses and sentences. Interpreters should pay attention to connecting words like "for, "therefore," or "but."

For example, Hebrews 12:1 reads, *"Therefore,* since we are surrounded by such a great cloud of witnesses, let us throw off everything that hinders and the sin that so easily entangles. And let us run with perseverance the race marked out for us" (NIV, emphasis added).

The word "therefore" is relating to the previous chapter in which Old Testament saints were regarded as those who had given a positive testimony or witness of faith. The phrase "cloud of witnesses" then would naturally refer back to the characters of the preceding chapter.[21]

Appendix D
Parsing Greek Verbs

Parsing Greek verbs has to do with determining person, tense and voice and mood. First, you'll need to determine the voice. Is it first person (I, we, us)? Is it second person (you, your, yours)? Or is it third person (we, they, theirs)? Next, ask if the verb is singular (S) or plural (P).

First, let's look at *tense*. Tense expresses time and/or duration of action.

- Present tense – Continuous, in the present

- Aorist tense – The action was finished in the past, with present continuing results

- Future tense – Action in the future

- Perfect tense – completed, with ongoing continuing results

- Imperfect tense – Continuous action in the past ("In the beginning was the Word, and the Word was with God, and the Word was God. He was in the beginning with God." – John 1:1-2).

Next is *voice*. Voice expresses the action as either completed by the subject of the verb or received by the subject. The subject either performs the action or is acted upon. There are three voices to look for:

- Active voice – ("But God *shows* his love for us..." – Romans 5:8)

- Passive voice – ("...but you *were sanctified*, you *were justified*..." – 1 Corinthians 6:11).

- Middle voice – (He *himself secured* eternal redemption." – Hebrew 9:12).

Next is *mood*, listed below. Mood expresses the writer's attitude toward the action.

- Indicative mood – A declaration of fact, a reality ("I glorified You on the earth." – John 17:4)

- Imperative – a command, a potential reality ("*Do not* quench the Spirit." – 1 Thessalonians 5:19)

- Subjunctive mood – Expresses uncertainty ("Therefore leaving the elementary teaching about the Christ, *let us* press on to maturity, not laying again a foundation of repentance from dead works and of faith toward God." – Heb. 6:1)

- Optative mood – Expresses a wish or desire. Is often introduced by "may."[15]

Many people are not the least bit excited about learning to parse Greek verbs. However, if you learn nothing else, become familiar with the present tense, and the imperative mood as they are frequently used in the New Testament. The present tense conveys a sense of continuous action or habitual practice, and the imperative mood indicates a command. This is especially important when you come across Paul's letters, with clear exhortations to believers.

APPENDIX E
BASIC GRAMMAR

"Consider what I say, for the Lord will give you understanding in everything." – 2 Timothy 2:7

I n 2 Timothy 2:7, Paul writes that the Lord will give understanding to those who consider His Word. Considering His word includes analyzing the grammatical function of a word in a phrase or sentence, which along with Greek and Hebrew word studies, helps determine a word's meaning.

Words in English can act as nouns, verbs, adjectives, or adverbs (among many other parts of speech). Take for example the word "back."

As a noun, "back" can mean the posterior part of a human or animal, support that you can lean against while sitting such as the back of a dental chair, or a person who plays in the back in football (among many other things).

As a verb, it can mean to travel in the opposite direction ("to go back"), to establish something as valid, as in "to back something up," or to support with financial backing.

As an adjective (describing a noun), it can refer to a location as in "the back entrance." As an adverb, modifying a verb, it can pertain to a former location or condition: "He went back to bed."

Knowing the basic parts of speech can be very helpful with biblical interpretation. Irving Jensen emphasizes the importance of word studies, writing that, "Just as a great door swings on small hinges, so the important theological statements of the Bible often depend upon even the smallest words, such as prepositions and articles."

A basic chart is included below.[11]

Part of Speech	Function	Examples from John, NKJV
Noun	Represents a person, place, thing, or idea	14:6 Jesus said to him, "I am the **way**, the **truth**, and the **life**. No one comes to the **Father** except through Me."
Pronoun	Takes the place of a noun	15:5 **I** am the vine, **you** are the branches. **He** who abides in **Me**, and **I** in **him**, bears much fruit; for without **Me you** can do nothing.
Adjective	Describes a noun or pronoun, tells what kind, which one, how many, etc.	3:16 For God so loved the world that He gave His **only begotten** Son, that whoever believes in Him should not perish but have **everlasting** life.
Article	Identifies something as indefinite or definite	8:35 And **a** slave does not abide in **the** house forever, but **a** son abides forever.
Verb	Represents an action or state of being	6:40 And this **is** the will of Him who **sent** Me, that everyone who **sees** the Son and **believes** in Him **may have** everlasting life; and I **will raise** him **up** at the last day.
Adverb	Typically describes a verb, but can modify a verb, adjective, or other adverb. Tells how, when, where, why, how often, or how much.	12:8 For the poor you have with you **always**, but Me you do not have **always**. 10:10 I have come that they may have life, and that they may have it **more abundantly**.

Preposition	Shows a relationship	1:3 All things were made **through** Him, and **without** Him nothing was made that was made.
Conjunction	Joins words, phrases, or clauses	4:21 **But** the hour is coming, **and** now is, when the true worshippers will worship the Father in spirit **and** truth; **for** the Father is seeking such to worship Him.
Interjection	Shows emotion or surprise, usually without grammatical connection to the rest of the sentence	Jer.32:17 **Ah** Lord GOD! **behold**, thou hast made heaven and earth by thy great power and outstretched arm, and there is nothing too hard for thee (KJV).

A NOTE ABOUT VERBS

The verb is the engine that drives a sentence or clause. The subject performs the action of the verb whereas the direct and indirect objects, if present, receive the action. Adverbs describe the action, and prepositional phrases may describe the action as well. Because verbs are so important, let's take more time to look at some grammatical concepts related to verbs, realizing that could be done with other parts of speech too.

Verb Tense

Verb tense specifies *when* the action occurred (past, present, or future) as well as kind of action (simple, complete, or ongoing). Considering verb tense when doing word studies will help you decide if the statement happened in the past, or will happen in the future (or both). The following chart breaks down the various verbal tenses you will find throughout Scripture:[11]

Verbal Terms	Function	Examples from Romans, ESV
Verb Tense	Specifies time of action (past, present, or future) as well as kind of action (simple, complete, or ongoing).	1:2 Which he **promised** beforehand through his prophets in the holy Scriptures. (Simple past, also called **preterit**, without reference to duration.)
Present	Indicates action or state in present time (may be simple or progressive, i.e. ongoing)	1:8 First, I **thank** my God through Jesus Christ for all of you, because your faith **is proclaimed** in all the world.
Past	Indicates action or state in past time (may be simple or progressive)	1:25 Because they **exchanged** the truth of God for a lie and **worshiped** and **served** the creature rather than the Creator, who is blessed forever! Amen.
Future	Indicates action or state in future time, uses will or shall as a helping verb, (again, may be simple or progressive)	11:26 And in this way all Israel **will be saved**, as it is written, "The Deliverer **will come** from Zion, he **will banish** ungodliness from Jacob."
Perfect	Makes a reference to a completed action in relation to present time	1:13 I want you to know, brothers, that I **have** often **intended** to come to you (but thus far **have been prevented**), in order that I may reap some harvest among you as well as among the rest of the Gentiles.
Past Perfect	Makes a reference to completed action in relation to past time, also called pluperfect	9:10 And not only so, but also when Rebecca **had conceived** children by one man, our forefather Isaac.

Future Perfect	Makes a reference to a completed action in relation to future time (a rare tense)	Mt.18:18 Assuredly I am saying to you, Whatever you forbid on earth, **shall have already been forbidden** in heaven. And whatever you permit on earth, **shall have already been permitted** in heaven (Wuest).
Progressive Form	Expresses continuous action in any tense except the perfect tenses	8:14 For as many as **are being** constantly **led** by God's Spirit, these are sons of God (Wuest).
Finite Verb	Any verb rendered with reference to time (excludes infinitives, participles, and gerunds)	8:15 You **did** not **receive** a spirit of slavery again with resulting fear... (Wuest).
Infinitive	A form of the verb that does not make reference to time, preceded by "to"	12:3 For by the grace given to me I say to everyone among you not **to think** of himself more highly than he ought **to think**, but **to think** with sober judgment, each according to the measure of faith that God has assigned.
Participle	A verbal adjective, it may also be used adverbially, in which case it "participates" in the action of a finite verb associated with it	12:6 **Having** gifts that differ according to the grace **given** to us, let us use them: if prophecy, in proportion to our faith.
Present Participle	Participle ending in "ing," also used with a helping verb to form progressives.	8:13 But, **assuming** that by the Spirit you are habitually **putting** to death the deeds of the body, you will live (Wuest).
Past Participle	Participle often ending in "ed," also used to form perfect tenses	7:5 For while we were living in the flesh, our sinful passions, **aroused** by the law, were at work in our members to bear fruit for death.

Gerund	A verb turned into a noun by adding "ing," common in English but not in Greek	8:19 For the creation waits with eager **longing** for the **revealing** of the sons of God.
Imperative	Used to express a command, sometimes formed by using *do, let, be*, or other helping verbs	12:2 **Do not be conformed** to this world, but **be transformed** by the renewal of your mind, that by testing you may discern what is the will of God, what is good and acceptable and perfect.
Subjunctive	Used to express a probable or possible action, not common in today's English except as expressed using modal auxiliary verbs	John 14:2 In my Father's house are many rooms. If it **were** not so, **would** I **have told** you that I go to prepare a place for you? (The use of *it were* is a true English subjunctive.)
Modal Auxiliary	Helping verbs that enable English verbs to express various shades of meaning, words like should, would, could, can, shall, must, may, and might. Look for these in the New Testament after the words *in order that* or *that*, where they help translate the Greek subjunctive in a purpose clause.	15:13 **May** the God of hope fill you with all joy and peace in believing, so that by the power of the Holy Spirit you **may** abound in hope. 6:1 **Should** we continue in sin that grace **may** abound? (Darby)
Active Voice	The subject performs the action of the verb or is in the state described.	5:8 But God **shows** his love for us in that while we **were** still sinners, Christ **died** for us.
Passive Voice	The subject of the verb is acted upon by an agent; look for the word by with the agent responsible for the action.	5:9 Since, therefore, we **have** now **been justified** by his blood, much more **shall** we **be saved** by him from the wrath of God.

Scott Duvall, Professor of New Testament at Ouachita Baptist University and author of *Grasping God's Word: A Hands-On Approach to Reading, Interpreting, and Applying the Bible*, says words are like pieces of a puzzle. According to Duvall, "They fit together to form a story or a paragraph in a letter (i.e., the big picture). Until you know the meaning of certain words, you will not be able to grasp the meaning of the whole passage. Not knowing the meaning of certain words in a passage of Scripture can be compared to the frustrating discovery that you don't have all the pieces to your puzzle. Like individual pieces of a puzzle, words bring the larger picture to life. Words are worth studying!" (Scott Duvall, *Grasping God's Word: A Hands-on Approach to Reading, Interpreting, and Applying the Bible*).

Though the legwork may seem intensive, the result brings joy in understanding of truth. The Lord will speak to you in the quietness of your soul as you move around those concordances and lexicons, and flip back and forth in your Bible as you cross-reference words. Soon, this "puzzle" will begin to connect and you will experience "aha!" moments that draw you into the powerful presence of God.

*"For no word from God will ever fail." – **Luke 1:37, NIV***

REFERENCES

1. "10 Biblical Reasons to Memorize Scripture." *Unlocking the Bible. N.p., 27 Mar. 2012. Web. 01 Nov. 2015. <http://www.unlockingthebible.org/reasons-memorize-scripture-bible/>.

2. "Application the Inductive Way." *RSS*. N.p., n.d. Web. 28 Oct. 2015. <http://www.biblestudymagazine.com/bible-study-magazine-blog/2015/2/19/application-the-inductive-way#sthash.S55ThCTK.dpuf>.

3. "Basic Hebrew Word Studies." *Basic Hebrew Word Studies*. N.p., n.d. Web. 06 Nov. 2015. <http://www.hebrew4christians.com/Grammar/Word_Studies/word_studies.html>.

4. "Bible Encyclopedia and Bible Study Tools." *Bible Study Tools*. N.p., n.d. Web. 03 Nov. 2015. <http://www.biblestudytools.com/encyclopedias/>.

5. "Bible Encyclopedia and Bible Study Tools." *Bible Study Tools.* N.p., n.d. Web. 03 Nov. 2015. <http://www.biblestudytools. com/encyclopedias/>.

6. "Bible Studies." *Inductive Bible Study System.* N.p., n.d. Web. 24 Oct. 2015. <http://www.intothyword.org/apps/ articles/?articleid=66163&columnid=3801>.

7. "Bible Studies." *STEP VII: APPLICATION!* N.p., n.d. Web. 28 Oct. 2015. <http://70030.netministry.com/apps/ articles/?articleid=31564&columnid=3801>.

8. "BiblicalStudies.org.uk: Figures of Speech in the Bible by Robert I Bradshaw." *BiblicalStudies.org.uk: Figures of Speech in the Bible by Robert I Bradshaw.* N.p., n.d. Web. 27 Oct. 2015. <http://biblicalstudies.org.uk/article_idioms.html>.

9. "Can We Trust the Greek New Testament?" *Can We Trust the Greek New Testament?* N.p., n.d. Web. 06 Nov. 2015. <http:// www.hebrew4christians.com/Articles/Jesus_Hebrew/ Greek_NT/greek_nt.html>

10. "Chapters and Verses in the Bible." *Precept Camden.* N.p., 11 Dec. 2009. Web. 24 Oct. 2015. <http://preceptcamden. com/2009/12/11/chapters-and-verses-in-the-bible/>.

11. "Explore the Bible on Your PDA or Smartphone." *Applying the Basics of English Grammar.* N.p., n.d. Web. 06 Nov. 2015. <https://www.olivetree.com/learningcenter/articles/grammar.php>.

12. "Extra-Biblical Sources Corroborate the Bible." N.p., n.d. Web. 2 Nov. 2015. <http://alwaysbeready.com/extrabiblical-historical-sources-corroborate-the-bible>.

13. "Extra-Biblical Sources Corroborate the Bible." N.p., n.d. Web. 2 Nov. 2015. <http://alwaysbeready.com/extrabiblical-historical-sources-corroborate-the-bible>.

14. "Facts and Figures | Dead Sea." *Dead Sea Facts and Figures Comments.* N.p., n.d. Web. 03 Nov. 2015. <http://dead-sea-wonder-of-nature.com/facts-and-figures/>.

15. "Greek Abbreviations." *Greek Abbreviations.* N.p., n.d. Web. 06 Nov. 2015. <http://www.preceptaustin.org/greek_abbreviations.htm>.

16. "Greek Word Studies." *Www.preceptaustin.org.* N.p., n.d. Web. 5 Nov. 2015. <http://www.preceptaustin.org/greek_word_studies1.htm>.

17. "How to Study Your Bible Inductively." Moody Bible Church, n.d. Web. 20 Oct. 2015. <http://www.moodychurch.org/static/uploads/sub_site_precept-bible-studies/orientationinductivebiblestudy>.

18. "Inductive Bible Study." *Inductive Bible Study.* N.p., n.d. Web. 24 Oct. 2015. < http://www.preceptaustin.org/inductive_bible_study.htm>.

19. "Inductive Bible Study: Interpretation." *Inductive Bible Study: Interpretation.* N.p., n.d. Web. 27 Oct. 2015. <http://www.preceptaustin.org/the_key_inductive_study_(pt2).htm>.

20. "Inductive Bible Study: Observation." *Inductive Bible Study: Observation.* N.p., n.d. Web. 24 Oct. 2015. < http://www.preceptaustin.org/observation.htm>.

21. "Lesson 6: Principles of Biblical Interpretation." *Bible.org.* N.p., n.d. Web. 09 Nov. 2015. <https://bible.org/seriespage/lesson-6-principles-biblical-interpretation>.

22. "Memorizing His Word." Memorizing His Word. N.p., n.d. Web. 18 Nov. 2015. <http://www.preceptaustin.org/Memorizing_His_Word.htm>.

23. "Rivermont Church of Christ." *Church of Christ.* N.p., n.d. Web. 09 Nov. 2015. <http://www.rmcoc.com/>.

24. "Six Principles For Interpreting Scripture." *Six Principles For Interpreting Scripture.* N.p., n.d. Web. 27 Oct. 2015. <http://rickwarren.org/devotional/english/six-principles-for-interpreting-scripture>.

25. "The Greeks Had a Word for It." *The Greeks Had a Word for It.* N.p., n.d. Web. 06 Nov. 2015. <http://www.raystedman.org/leadership/smith/ch10.html>.

26. "The Historical Books of the New Testament." *Bible.org.* N.p., n.d. Web. 09 Nov. 2015. <https://bible.org/seriespage/3-historical-books-new-testament>.

27. "Tour of the Bible, Part 2: The Historical Books | Bible Gateway Blog." *Tour of the Bible, Part 2: The Historical Books | Bible Gateway Blog.* N.p., n.d. Web. 09 Nov. 2015. <https://www.biblegateway.com/blog/2011/02/tour-of-the-bible-part-2-the-historical-books/>.

28. "Typology-Study of Types." *Typology-Study of Types.* N.p., n.d. Web. 18 Nov. 2015. <http://www.preceptaustin.org/typology-study_of_types.htm#b>.

29. "We Recommend the Inductive Bible Study Method That Has Five Major Steps." *We Recommend the Inductive Bible Study Method That Has Five Major Steps*. N.p., n.d. Web. 27 Oct. 2015. <http://www.backdoorbible.org/html/inductive_bible_study.htm>.

30. "Why Is Bible Memorization Important?" *GotQuestions.org*. N.p., n.d. Web. 01 Nov. 2015. <http://www.gotquestions.org/Bible-memorization.html>.

31. "Why Is Bible Memorization Important?" *GotQuestions.org*. N.p., n.d. Web. 01 Nov. 2015. <http://www.gotquestions.org/Bible-memorization.html>.

32. "Why Use a Bible Dictionary?" *Do Not Depart*. N.p., n.d. Web. 03 Nov. 2015. <http://donotdepart.com/why-use-a-bible-dictionary>.

33. Arthur, Kay. *How to Study Your Bible*. Eugene, Or.: Harvest House, 1994. Print.

34. *BibleGateway.com: A Searchable Online Bible in over 100 Versions and 50 Languages*. N.p., n.d. Web. 24 Oct. 2015. <https://www.biblegateway.com/>.

35. Epstein, Isidore. *The Babylonian Talmud.* New York: R. Bennett, 1959. Print. Sanhedrin 43a

36. Epstein, Isidore. *The Babylonian Talmud.* New York: R. Bennett, 1959. Print. Sanhedrin 43a

37. *ESV. English Standard Version Containing the Old and New Testament. The Holy Bible.* Wheaton, IL: Crossway Bibles, 2001. Print.

38. Kang, Joshua Choonmin. *Scripture by Heart: Devotional Practices for Memorizing God's Word.* Downers Grove, IL: IVP, 2010. Print.

39. *KJV. Authorized King James Version. The Holy Bible.* Nashville, TN: Broadman & Holman, 1987. Print.

40. Lockhart, Clinton. *Principles of Interpretation: As Recognized Generally by Biblical Scholars, Treated as a Science, Derived Inductively from an Exegesis of Many Passages of Scripture.* Fort Worth: S.H. Taylor, 1915. Print.

41. *MSG.* Peterson, Eugene H. *The Message.* Colorado Springs, CO: NavPress, 2004. Print.

42. *NIV. New International Version. The Holy Bible.* Colorado Springs, CO: Biblica, 2011. Print.

43. *NLT. New Living Translation. The Holy Bible.* Wheaton, IL: Tyndale House, 1996. Print.

44. Piper, John. "Why Memorize Scripture?" *Desiring God.* N.p., 5 Sept. 2096. Web. 1 Nov. 2015. <http://www.desiringgod. org/articles/why-memorize-scripture>.

45. Shirock, Robert J. *Transformed by the Renewing of Your Mind.* Plymoth, MI: Jubilee, LLC, 2008. Print.

46. Sire, James W. *Scripture Twisting: 20 Ways the Cults Misread the Bible.* Downers Grove, IL: InterVarsity, 1980. Print.

47. Strobel, Lee. *The Case for the Real Jesus: A Journalist Investigates Current Attacks on the Identity of Christ.* Grand Rapids, MI: Zondervan, 2007. Print.

48. *TLB. The Living Bible.* Wheaton, IL: Tyndale House, 1971. Print.

49. Traina, Robert A. *Methodical Bible Study: A New Approach to Hermeneutics.* Ridgefield Park? N.J.: Biblical Seminary in New York, 1952. Print.

50. Walvoord, John F. *The Prophecy Knowledge Handbook.* Wheaton, IL: Victor, 1990. Print.

ABOUT THE AUTHOR

H enry Jackson III, a bondservant of Jesus Christ. He is a native of Memphis, TN, who now calls Atlanta, GA his home. Henry primarily utilizes his spiritual gifts of teaching and leadership at Elizabeth Baptist Church in Atlanta, GA, where he currently serves as the Children & Youth Spiritual Formation Director. Henry enjoys spending time with his darling wife Vanessa and son Henry IV, kayaking, racquetball, and mountain-bike riding.

Henry is the founder of Inductive Bible Study LLC, an organization that empowers individuals to grow in their faith by enabling them to study the Bible inductively using their favorite mobile device. Find out more at InductiveBibleStudyApp.com.

As a Myasthenia Gravis (MG) survivor, Henry is a living testimony of God's healing power. Each day that God gives him the strength, he is constantly pursuing ways to glorify God and to make Him known to the world. A portion of the proceeds from the sale of this book will be donated to the Myasthenia Gravis Foundation of America, Inc. Find out more at www.myasthenia.org.

Made in the USA
Columbia, SC
22 January 2018